REAL RIDING

How to Ride in Harmony with Horses

REAL RIDING

How to Ride in Harmony with Horses

PERRY WOOD

KENILWORTH PRESS

This book is dedicated to any fellow pilgrims seeking
'the truth' about horsemanship (and if you find it before I do,
can you let me know, please?)

First published in Great Britain 2002 by
Kenilworth Press
Addington
Buckingham
MK18 2JR

Disclaimer of Liability
The author and publisher shall have neither liability nor responsibility to any person or entity
with respect to any loss or damage caused or alleged to be caused directly or indirectly by the
information contained in this book. While the book is as accurate as the authors can make it,
there may be errors, omissions and inaccuracies.

British Library Cataloguing in Publication Data
A CIP record for this book is available from the British Library

ISBN 1-872119-51-4

Text design by Paul Saunders
Typesetting and layout by Kenilworth Press
Printed and bound in Great Britain by Bell & Bain, Glasgow

Contents

Part 1: Horsework

The underlying reasons why we are drawn to horses, why they touch
our souls. What they can do for us in terms of developing ourselves
as individuals. Looking at the recreational role horses now play in our
society and why it is important to seek to achieve harmony with these
wonderful creatures.

1. All horses are big and strong
2. Horses are not machines
3. Horses react first and think later
4. Horses are emotional creatures with busy social lives
5. Horses are cleverer than you think
6. Horses were not created to carry a rider
7. Horses are sensitive to pain and discomfort
8. Horses are not human beings
9. Every horse is unique

Part 2: Riderwork

Looking at aspects and details of how to sit properly in the saddle. How
to find a way to ride with true balance. Centres of gravity. Importance of
looking ahead. Softness and allowing movement of the horse's back.
Developing a sense of feel and harmony.

Part 4: Partnership Work

Part 5: Horsemanship Work

Acknowledgements

My sincere thanks to family, friends and loved ones for their faith and support, particularly when I appear to be doing odd things, making a fool of myself or making apparently crazy changes of direction: things always turn out better than expected in the end, hey!

Thanks to the two- and four-legged folks whom I feel have made a real difference to me in my horsemanship thus far: Colonel Mario de Mendoca, for a sound foundation in the classical principles; Erik Herbermann, for a dedication to 'the truth' and for pointing out that I'd had a frontal lobotomy; Danny Pevsner. for showing me the power of 'releasing', of being soft and applying the Alexander Technique to riding in an ever-expanding way; Steph, for introducing me to 'natural horsemanship' ten years before most people had heard of it; Kate Parkes for her wisdom and showing me that the Alexander technique goes way beyond the physical.

But mostly, thanks to the following, who are the **real** teachers: Puffin, Rambler, Fleur, William, Bacardi, Sweep, George, Mr Tibbs, Lobby, Esaya, Monte, Charity, Hawk, Nissan, Doric, another William, Indie, Fabulous, Safar, Pinkie (Mirage), Donk (Fantastique), Plum, Flash, Hannah, Arnie, Little Sister, Corsaro, Momma, Tabu, Magpie, Andante, Rebel, Spider, Bananas, Treacle, Ebony, Serendipity, Legend, Major, Magnum, Jet, the twins, Goose, Ivy, Mustard, Jerry, Ollie, Precious Vision, Kensa, Shah, Nightshade, Banshee, Tchewy, Mythos, Drum, Europa, Princess Leah, Soti, Bourneville and many other noble horses too numerous to mention.

Thanks to all my pupils over the years: you thought I was teaching you (hopefully), but actually you have taught me far more!

Thanks to Vanessa Brookham, for telling me I 'must' write this book in the first place.

Huge thanks to Lesley, David, Dee and all at Kenilworth Press for their courage, missionary zeal, insight, professionalism and encouragement in preparing, editing and publishing this book – I feel genuinely lucky to be working with you guys.

PERRY WOOD

Author's note

It is my hope that this book will make a real difference to you and your riding, and therefore to the horses you ride.

In writing this book I do not claim that this is the 'right' way or the 'only' way. Nobody has all the answers: every horse, every moment and every rider is unique, so the answers are forever changing. It is up to you to find out what is appropriate in each circumstance – that is one of the things that keeps horses interesting. Just following this book to the letter, or any other source of instruction, will not necessarily work in every situation. That doesn't mean I don't believe in the principles and ideas I have set out here – they are all discoveries that have given me some fantastic moments with horses, and I hope they will work just as well for you.

What I wish to give you in this book are new ways of approaching horses and your riding, empowering ways to progress and alternative attitudes and ways to view horses and riding that you may not have looked into before.

Good luck with your riding.

Prelude

Just imagine…

Imagine being taken from your mother at six months old.

Imagine being tied to a wall by your head.

Imagine being loved so much, and not being understood at all.

Imagine having your top lip twisted to make you behave.

Imagine being bought and sold as a slave.

Imagine having no say in what you do or where you live.

Imagine committing no crime, but spending up to twenty-three hours a day in a cell.

Imagine having a hunk of metal (with a joint that pinches) in your mouth.

Imagine being pulled and yanked around by that hunk of metal.

Imagine being kicked in the ribs every day.

Imagine being taken from friends and family.

Imagine having your feet grabbed, hammered and burned.

Imagine being made to run in circles until you are sore.

Imagine someone bouncing around on your back.

Imagine being forced to do 'ballet'.

Imagine being made to run flat out until your lungs burn and your legs go weak, then being whipped to run faster.

Imagine having your head tied down.

Imagine being forced to do the high-jump, and being whipped for being unable or unwilling.

Imagine being loaded onto a truck with strangers and the smell of death, and ending up in a can of pet food.

Sounds pretty heavy, eh?

Sorry about that, but it makes you think ...

Well, that's the serious stuff out of the way. There is no doubt that riding/horsemanship is an art, but that doesn't mean it has to be all frustration, confusion, misery and mystery. **Real Riding** is intentionally light-hearted, and contains lots of amusing things to do both on and off the horse.

It works for me, I hope it works for you.

Part 1

Horsework

To be really effective with horses and to experience fine riding, it is essential to develop a depth of knowledge and a feel for the true nature of horses. It is only by accepting the horse's nature and working *with* Nature that great results and moments of real unity can happen.

Horses are fascinating creatures, far more complex than people sometimes realise: sensitive, communicative, emotional, intelligent, loving, defensive, quick-witted, noble, gentle and wild. The more time we spend understanding the horse's nature, the easier it is to find the answers to the constant stream of questions and challenges that come along as we work with these wonderful beings.

A horse is a horse is a horse: that is the real raw material with which we are choosing to work when we ride.

In this section we will explore the horse's nature and look at ways in which to become more effective by working with that nature.

Horses are totally amazing!

If you're reading this book, you probably love horses and think they are totally amazing … perfectly understandable, but why? What is it about horses that attracts so many people to them, that makes us put up with so much discomfort, heartache, frustration, shortage of cash, hideous weather and personal danger, and invest so much time in the bizarre pastime of riding?

Horses have been admired throughout the history of mankind for their wonderful qualities; they have been portrayed in art and mythology, praised in literature. and even revered in great holy works such as the Bible and the Koran, so it shouldn't be surprising that so many of us here in the twenty-first century have caught the 'horse-bug!'

Horses mean different things to different people, but most agree that the horse is a noble, forgiving, beautiful, gentle, thrilling, powerful, graceful, sensitive, awe-inspiring, patient, challenging and exciting creature to have around. That's an impressive list: if you knew a person who fitted all those descriptions I'd say you were totally smitten and helplessly in love!

Let's just add the flip side of the horse's qualities while we're here: horses are also dangerous, uncomfortable, frustrating, unpredictable, expensive, hard work, over-sensitive, insensitive, neurotic and smelly! (Well, maybe it wasn't true love after all.)

Now that we have entered the twenty-first century, we have an incredible opportunity to forge a special relationship with horses, Nature and ultimately ourselves. And why? Because, the role of the horse in the western world is almost entirely recreational. This allows us to relate to these incredible creatures on a 'higher' level, and to gain more, much more, from our relationship with them than in the days when they were primarily needed for our livelihood.

However, along with this opportunity to share something 'higher' with horses comes a responsibility, and that is to do the utmost to understand the horse's needs, physically, mentally and emotionally. Our responsibilities to the horse can only be fulfilled by controlling ourselves, by gaining more understanding of the horse and by learning to work within the laws of nature.

Despite our highest intentions, the horse's life is often filled with fear, discomfort, and misunderstanding. This is a prime motivation for writing this book and for doing the work that I do. It is my hope that it will make a difference, not only to riders, but also to the horses themselves: they deserve it. I sincerely hope you agree.

Our link with Nature

The more technologically advanced our everyday lives become, the more popular it becomes to ride horses and spend time around them. Could it be that horses give us the direct link with Nature that we need and have lost in our modern lives?

Although people think of horses as being 'domesticated', little has really been done in evolutionary terms to take away the horse's true nature and instinct for survival. When they are born, foals don't pop out of the womb human-friendly, ready to wear tack or be led by a halter; they are fundamentally feral, and they normally try to leg it!

So even the domesticated horse is still an animal of pure 'Nature'. The fact that we can learn to relate to horses, be with them, share experiences with them, sit on them and borrow their natural reactions for flight, gives us a direct link to Nature itself, and since we are also creatures of Nature, linking up with horses helps to put us back in touch with ourselves. (Whoa, this is getting a bit deep ...)

> Let's go over that again. Communicating with horses is communicating with pure Nature. Since we are a part of Nature, communicating with horses can put us back in touch with ourselves. Wow!

Face to face with ourselves

In no other situation are people so hypersensitive about being questioned or criticised as when they are riding a horse. You can tell someone they ride a push-bike worse than a dog, but say the slightest thing about the way they are riding and it's as if you have thrust a knife into their very soul! Perhaps this is because, underneath, we know that when we are dealing with or communicating with horses, we are dealing with a reflection of our own inner self, and that is why it is so important for us to feel that our communicating or treating of the horse is in a just and fair manner.

A great gift

It's a funny thing, but we always seem to get the horse that teaches us the very thing we need to learn.

Against the underlying desire to reconnect with Nature and prove ourselves 'worthy' to the horse, things can become pretty testing for us, not least because we can always rely on horses to bring out the weakest link in our personality!

The fact that being around horses tests our individual weaknesses is a great gift, since having attention drawn to our shortcomings, however annoying or unpleasant it may feel, means that we become aware of them and can do something to improve ourselves. Whether the shortcomings are self-doubt, lack of patience, lack of focus, being over-bearing, heavy-handedness, being weak-willed or whatever, the horse will surely bring it to the surface for you to examine and require you to fix it before you can proceed very much further into the game of horsemanship.

So there you are: a horse is not only good fun, it is also a beautiful-looking psychotherapist who lives on grass and doesn't charge by the hour!

Horses are so forgiving

Fixing our personal shortcomings is not easy, so one of the other great things about horses is their willingness to forgive and keep forgiving. While we bumble about making an mess of everything, repeating the same mistakes over and over again and trying to sort ourselves out, they forgive and forgive and forgive in order to let us have yet another try.

Time and time again horses will forgive unjust or clumsy handling. If you were seven feet tall, fast as lightning, strong as a horse and weighed 500kg, would you put up with some of the stuff horses put up with? I know I wouldn't: in fact I don't, and I'm much weedier!

Domination and force

Because horses are such forgiving and naturally passive creatures, it can be so easy to slip into using force or domination to impress our will onto the animal. This is a trap that is ever-present.

Sometimes we feel that there is no other way than to resort to force, but most likely there is another way and it is just that we haven't become skilled enough to discover it yet.

'Sell it and buy another!'

Another alternative to coming face to face with ourselves and learning to grow as a result of being with horses is this: sell it and buy another one! Sometimes it is better to sell a horse on to someone with more skill and experience, but sometimes the horse that won't do 'this or that' for a person is the very horse to teach them the thing they most need to learn. What happens so frequently (and you may well have seen this) is that Mr X will sell a horse because it has a certain behaviour trait, then three months down the line his new horse will start showing exactly the same behaviour trait as the last one! So what does Mr X do? He sells it and buys yet one, which starts doing the same! Will he ever be a great horseman? Will politicians ever stop lying? Will pigs learn to fly by the end of this week?

Never-ending challenges

Wouldn't it be a little boring if everything went well all the time? There isn't much chance of that where horses are concerned. Let's be honest, most humans like a challenge, and no one more so than horse people: people who

Imagine you're a horse...

You have an innate and total sense of justice.

To lead through respect, rather than fear:

1. Be focused, without having tunnel vision.

2. Notice when the horse 'tries' for you.

3. Praise a lot.

4. Be self-confident without being egotistical

... well, that sounds easy (not!)

don't like a challenge ride bicycles or lawnmowers instead of horses and don't get any nearer to horses than looking at them over a field gate or at photos of fancy-maned Arabians and Andalusians on calendars.

Overcoming challenges by perseverance, physical skill, mindpower and fair means is one of the ultimate ways for a person to experience real satisfaction: horses almost constantly offer us that opportunity.

The wonderful thing about the challenges that horses present to us is the fact that these challenges happen on all sorts of different levels.

To be really good with horses we need to hone our physical skills, learning a high degree of body awareness and body control. Not just learning to do precise things with different parts of our bodies simultaneously, like rubbing your tummy and patting your head at the same time, but learning the often more difficult skill of doing almost nothing at all whilst the horse's movement bounces us around.

We also need to learn a great deal of mental control, learning to be a positive and just leader, learning self-control in the face of fear and frustration, thinking of effective ways to communicate with an 'alien' creature, learning to be patient, and learning to think our way around sometimes insurmountable problems (cor blimey!). This is real character-building stuff and it is difficult to go near horses for much time at all before some of these issues come up and require us to face them.

The path of learning, experiences and challenges offered to us by horses is never-ending. You could spend your whole life dedicated to becoming great with horses and there would still be another horse turn up that would be a challenge for you or have something new to teach you. This is another reason why horses are amazing: they can keep it interesting for a whole lifetime, and then some!

Things to do...

1. Appreciate the horse not only as a source of fun, but also as a way to show you things about yourself – being a better horseman might help in other areas of your life. For example, developing an ability to have more self-control with the horse may help you to have the same control whilst sitting in traffic or when things aren't going well for you at home or at work.

2. Enjoy the challenges that horses present to you as exactly that: challenges. Overcoming challenges can be very rewarding. Challenges

always bring a gift along with them; see if you can find the gift in the challenge and the whole thing will become fun instead of difficult. **Always avoid over-challenging yourself, as this is not only unhelpful to you, it also often results in the horse suffering too.**

3. Appreciate the fact that the horse is a forgiving creature. Let him know you appreciate his patience when you can't get something right.

4. Read as many books as possible on the horse's nature (especially while commuting to work or while having lunch at work in the city).

5. Spend as much time as possible around horses. Watch horses in the field and observe what they get up to. What do they do with each other? What do they do with their time? What do they do differently from each other? How does each horse fit in and socialise? What is each horse like with other people? Which ones are playful? Which ones are independent? Which ones are leaders? Which are bullies? Which are loving? Which are wind-up merchants? Which are dozy? Which are intelligent? Which are mentally challenged? Which are hyper? And watch **HOW** they do the things they do. Get youself into **HORSE MODE.**

Quick reference...

Horses are a challenge; horsemanship requires mental skills as much as physical ones; be totally open-minded; horses are pure Nature; they bring us face to face with ourselves; to be a master requires understanding of the horse's nature; horsemanship is a very broad subject; horses are very forgiving.

Chapter 2

Nine ridiculously obvious facts about horses

1. All horses are big and strong

However obvious that may seem, it is important to remember the spindly size of our arms compared to the size of the horse's neck: forget strength, there is no contest! Increase your skill, knowledge, feel and timing to guide the horse to your way of thinking.

Most horses just don't realise how big and strong they are in relation to humans, but see themselves as a very edible morsel about the size of a chicken kebab or a hamster. This is a very, **VERY** fortunate aspect of their nature for us. Things only start falling apart when our behaviour shows the horse the extent of his size and power.

2. Horses are not machines, they have minds of their own

About the only similarities between machines and horses are that they can both wear out and they will both do what you ask if you know how to work them properly.

When you press a 'button' on a horse and don't get the reaction you want, it may be that:

► The horse hasn't understood your request.

► You haven't asked clearly or properly.

► The horse would rather be doing something else, somewhere else.

► He wasn't listening anyway.

► He is not physically capable of carrying out your request, or would find it physically uncomfortable to do so even though he understood: this is important.

► The horse is not sure you are worthy of the respect necessary for him to do your will (he's sticking a hoof up at you).

When you press a button on a machine and don't get the reaction you want, it may be that:

► It's bust!

► You pressed the wrong button.

► It's not switched on.

That's it!

3. Horses react first and think later

Imagine spending much of your life thinking you may be about to get killed and eaten. To say you'd be 'a bit on your toes' is an understatement.

Somewhere in every horse's mind is this ever-present thought, which instinctively makes him react with lightning speed to whatever he sees as a potential threat. Horses can react so fast that they don't have time to think – so what chance does a rider have of keeping up with them? The chance is sometimes a pretty slim one.

Imagine you're a horse...

You almost always behave in a way that reflects your desire for self-preservation.

Remember: the horse's body expresses his emotions – sometimes in a very big way.

We have all seen film footage of a zebra (a stripy horse) being chased by lions. The zebra runs like hell for a certain distance, then stops, turns around and has a look back to see if it really was a lion. If the zebra had stopped and had a look before it ran, it may have been the lion's dinner. This is exactly why horses are suspicious of anything new, and why they react first and think later.

Horses react to each other, and most particularly to their herd leader: if the herd leader says something is OK then it probably is. It is our responsibility to be that trustworthy herd leader; to be there for the horse at all times.

4. *Horses are emotional creatures with busy social lives*

Because horses totally rely on being in a group for their personal survival, they have evolved complex relationships. Since we humans also rely on being part of a group for our survival, we too have developed complex relationships – bonds of love, friendships, strong family ties, hierarchies, associates – and all manner of ways to communicate with each other in similar ways to horses. The fact that horses naturally have these relationships within their society just as we do, means that we can easily tap into this aspect of their nature in many different ways.

Unlike dogs, horses have a constantly fluid pecking order (hierarchy). This means that they are always thinking about trying to move up the promotional ladder. Because that is part of how horses naturally treat each other, they try to do the same with us. Like another horse, they can see us as either the little guy that always gets pushed around and beaten up, or the bully who nobody likes because he beats everyone else up, or the calm, admirable leader whom they respect and trust, or one of the followers in between.

Respect, trust and how to get it

DO

► Look sure of yourself.

► Be calm in a crisis.

► Be kind, but don't be a wimp or a pushover.

► Be a colourful character and keep life interesting – boring leaders don't usually last long in government because they don't inspire their followers.

► Achieve an independent seat – i.e. ride with balance alone, without having to grip with your legs or hands.

► Listen to everything the horse is telling you when you are on the ground, in the stable, in the paddock or on his back – leaders who don't listen to their followers are not popular for long.

► Be competent at things without 'showing off'.

► Move in a confident, smooth and effective way, not jerky, apologetic, wimpy, snappy or hyper.

► Smile a lot.

► Praise and reward the horse much more often than you'd think necessary.

► Ask for a little and be pleased: sometimes you ask for a little and get a lot.

► Look at things from the horse's point of view.

► Treat the horse with respect for his strength, gentleness, willingness, heart and soul.

► Become aware of your body language and what it is saying to the horse.

► Give the horse lots of rest between requests.

► Let him know every time he is doing something right.

DON'T

► Cause pain or discomfort.

► Let horses walk into your space.

► Appear afraid or fazed by anything.

► Loose your temper, get impatient or angry.

► Ask for too much.

► Act heavy handed or uncoordinated.

► Talk yourself down.

► Act like an incompetent, even if you feel like one!

5. Horses are cleverer than you think

Many people say horses can't be that intelligent or they wouldn't let us ride them: but if we're that intelligent, how come we go to work every day, sit in traffic, pay a mortgage, elect incompetent governments, fight wars, watch TV, ride unpredictable herbivores for 'fun' and feel obliged to spend Christmas with our relatives?

The funny thing about the horse's intelligence is that the more you look for it, the more you see it in action. The opposite is also true: many horse people talk about how small the horse's brain is and how horses are as 'thick as a brick', but they are only judging it from their own subjective viewpoint in human terms. Actually, horses are very clever at being horses. Often when horses appear to be thick, they are trying to tell the dumb human something, and from the horse's point of view the dumb human just isn't listening in the right way!

Remember: a horse is not a dumb animal!

The horse's memory capacity is phenomenal. It is part of his survival mechanism. The combination of the horse's memory and his enjoyment of habit are both essential aspects of training the horse. Before losing your temper, punishing or doing anything unwise with a horse, don't forget that he won't forget – which means that you may be making more work for yourself in the future, setting back the progress you have made together and throwing away the respect and trust he has built up for you. Horses remember emotionally charged experiences with more clarity than they do unemotional events, so something scary will have more of an effect in the future than something dull and boring.

> If a horse does something three times, it can become a habit.

Remember: horses always remember!

It takes about three repetitions of something for a horse to log it into his memory and make something a habit: bear that in mind as you structure the riding you do. It is all about common sense and being intelligent all the time while you ride.

6. Horses were not created to carry a rider

In evolutionary terms we have been riding horses for only a nano-second of time (opinions disagree, but about six thousand years). The process of evolution normally takes place over millions of years, although experts now believe that animals develop and evolve in fits and starts. Even allowing for the idea that animals can evolve quickly, six thousand years is very little time in which to develop the horse physically or mentally from its original feral state as a nomadic, foraging prey animal, into a beast that can easily carry a man on its back. There is no doubt that we have bred horses to be stronger and more suitable for our purposes, but there is still a long way to go (probably millennia) before horses fully evolve to carry a rider.

Horses need us be sensitive to the fact that they have delicate backs, so we should learn to sit as 'well' as we can. It is also important to consider physical pain as a very common source of apparent behaviour problems (or 'playing up') in the horse.

7. *Horses are sensitive to pain and discomfort*

Despite horses' size and frequently apparent insensitivity, one of the characteristics that enable us to ride them is their high level of physical sensitivity. Any animal that can flick a fly off its skin, as horses can, has to be sensitive. As well as the advantages, many difficulties that we have with horses also stem from the fact that they are so incredibly sensitive, not only physically but mentally and emotionally too.

> Horses are always in the NOW.

Paradoxically, although they are very sensitive, emotionally excited or scared horses will instinctively move into pressure and push against something 'solid' or even uncomfortable for all they're worth.

The fact is, that whoever you are and at whatever level you are riding, every time you ride a horse you are either training it or un-training it: you make horses either more or less responsive by your actions. (Yikes, that sounds like a real responsibility.)

There are three areas for us to consider here:

1. How to make horses more sensitive (to the aids).

2. How to make horses less sensitive, when required.

3. Recognising when we are causing discomfort to the horse without meaning to, and how to avoid doing so.

Remember, it is mostly animals that hunt for food who give food to each other as reward, comfort or tokens of love – animals such as dogs and humans. Horses never give each other gifts of food as reward. They just give each other friendship, safety and a bit of peace ... that is the horse's natural comfort zone. So this is a valuable tool for us to use in training and riding, since the horse naturally understands it, whereas rewarding with food is a less direct form of approval to a horse, even though he seems to like it and we enjoy feeding him.

The horse must always be able to choose a way out of discomfort.

8. Horses are not human beings

Many people make the mistake of assuming that horses think in 'English', or understand our human ways of seeing things. It is important to realise that, although horses are not dumb and share many thoughts and emotions with us, they have quite a different angle on life; but then again, we humans have wildly different angles on life from one another, hence the success of books like *Men are from Mars, Women are from Venus* (the reading of which makes me marvel at the fact that we ever manage to communicate or procreate at all, let alone with an entirely different species!).

There is a gap between the way we humans and horses see the world, and it is up to us, not the horse, to try to bridge that gap – not by shouting louder, but by understanding the horse's view. Horses are not very clever at speaking/understanding English or at being human: humans are not very good at speaking/understanding 'Equus' or at being horses! Start thinking in 'Equus' and not in English to get great results with horses.

Remember: a horse does not think in English!

9. Every horse is unique

Well, that seems pretty obvious, but it's amazing how easy it is to forget that every horse is different and unique. All too easily we make assumptions and do not get the best from each horse; worse still, we treat every horse the same and 'come a real cropper'.

Even horses that are full sisters and brothers are surprisingly individual. This is a very important fact to bear in mind when you get on a horse you don't know well. It may be a familiar height, build and colour, but it will have had its own unique experiences, will feel and respond in a slightly different way to every other horse you've ridden, and will have its own little idiosyncrasies.

Expect the unexpected when you are around horses.

That's why it is important to have no expectations when you get on a horse you don't know well; let's face it, even a horse you know well can surprise you!

To really understand horses, you need to try out as many as possible. Riding lots of different horses is a good idea, and not just different horses in the same indoor school, but in different situations. Riding horses of different ages is also a great way to gain experience. Youngsters are especially interesting to ride, as they don't make many assumptions or do much guesswork as to what you are asking like older horses do.

NB: It is important not to be over-horsed or take risks when riding different horses.

► Learn to quickly notice each horse's individual characteristics.

► Assume that all horses are perfect; they're just waiting for the rider to be perfect in order to display that fact!

► Remember that many human relationships suffer because one partner wants to change the other too much; horses are usually more willing to change than human partners, but there are limits!

Part 2

Riderwork

In this section you will learn what it takes to ride like a dream.

You will learn about the powerful benefits of keeping it simple, sitting correctly, staying in balance using softness and quietness so that riding becomes easier and more rewarding, for both horse and rider.

Sitting in the saddle with graceful poise and communicating with well-timed, subtly applied aids is well within the reach of every rider.

Horses mirror their riders: as you sit more beautifully, so you enable the horse to carry himself more beautifully ... this is **real riding**.

Chapter 3

True balance: standing up with a horse between your legs!

There is much information and lots of opinions on the minutiae of the riding seat and position in books, and it can be a little confusing, but as one of my early riding masters said, 'Meester Wood, you should seemply have your berm in zee saddle!' The simple fact is that the better your seat and position in the saddle, the better horses will go for you, the less of a struggle it all becomes and the more mysteriously effortless it appears to the onlooker.

There are basically two types of seat: the full (classical), and the forward (jumping) seats. Ideally you learn both. Despite its natural appearance when mastered, the full seat is more difficult to learn and takes longer to acquire. Time spent acquiring a good seat, position and posture on horseback is never wasted: in fact, taking the time is the quickest way to become any good; there are no short-cuts. At the end of the day there are as many different seats as there are people who sit on a horse, but there are some important classical guidelines to help.

What makes the riding seat so tricky to master is the changeable, unpredictable nature of the beast underneath you, and the fact that the harder you try, the harder it gets. Please don't be put off – that's what makes it so interesting.

THE BENEFITS of sitting correctly are:

1. You're more likely to stay on!

2. The aids become more effective and lighter.

Imagine you're a horse...

You have a highly developed sense of body awareness: your body is your major way of expressing your thoughts and feelings.

3. Sluggish horses go more willingly, and ...

4. ... forward-going horses are less likely to run off with you.

5. You won't get so many aches and pains as from sitting crookedly, with grip, bent over or out of balance.

6. Horses will be more comfortable, happier about carrying you, and less likely to get back problems.

7. You will look good on a horse (always important, I believe)!

8. The horse and you start to become one centaur-like being, the ultimate union with the horse.

Standing up?

The title of this chapter is significant. The terms riding **SEAT** and **SITTING** on the horse commonly mislead people into thinking that being on a horse is like being in a chair, i.e. with their legs in front of their buttocks. The key to both the forward (jumping) seat and the full seat is to be in perfect vertical balance, i.e. if the horse were instantly to become anti-matter and disappear into a parallel universe, the rider would land feet-first on the ground, and not fall over. As with much of riding, this is sometimes easier said than done. Although the position is one of 'standing up', it is still ideal to allow your full weight to be on the saddle (during the sitting aspects of riding).

One of the hardest, yet most worthwhile things a rider can learn to do on a horse is to do NOTHING incredibly well, especially in trot and canter

Ten-point guide to a better seat

1. 'Feel' your point of balance.

2. Look where you want to go – perferably ahead, between the horse's ears!

3. Think of sitting tall, your head floating upwards (rather than trying to sit up straight like a sergeant major). Keep it easy and simple.

4. Allow your legs to fall away from your body.

5. Have straight wrists and hands, but softly.

6. Stay very relaxed in your waist and buttocks, without collapsing.

7. Maintain the lightest pressure on the stirrups, with a gently lowered heel.

8. Let your body be 'soft' inside, from the top of your head to your heels.

9. Allow your chest to be relaxed, and breathe freely down into your body.

10. Relax your jaw and tongue: smile a little.

Gravity and balance

> The ultimate aim is to ride by balance alone.

The ultimate aim is to ride by balance alone, with absolutely no gripping up whatsoever. Many people ride for years without finding true balance on a horse. True balance is a very tiny place to find, so it is not surprising that we find all kinds of ways to compensate and fool ourselves into thinking we have achieved it.

Of course, the level of balance required to stay on a bouncing, moving, slightly unpredictable animal is considerable and takes a good deal of practice. But that practice needs to be the right kind of practice. Unfortunately we can become quite brilliant at riding without balance by years of the wrong kind of practice!

► Many twentieth-century riders were taught to ride by gripping with their knees. This is often referred to as an old-fashioned approach, but it is quite a recent invention. Riding with 'grip' actually contributes towards squeezing the rider out of the saddle. (You'll find more about this in Chapter 4, 'Legs, legs, legs!')

► **Unless your upper body is precisely upright over your lower body, you will not be riding with balance. It is common to see competent riders riding with their upper body slightly behind the vertical. This is not true balance and causes compensatory stiffening of the stomach or thigh muscles, which affects the brilliance, freedom and forwardness of the horse's movement. True balance allows you to let go of your body and legs completely, and still maintain poise in the saddle.**

► The horse's centre of gravity is inside his chest, below and just behind the wither. The human's centre of gravity is just below the navel, between the hips. The nearer the horse's and the rider's centres of gravity come towards each other, the more unity is possible between the two beings.

Horses are stronger, bigger and faster than we are. So forget about using physical power, and learn to sit well and use your brain instead!

▶ Think of sitting in the front of the saddle, not pushing forwards hard with the seat, as that benefits neither partner, but with the idea of carrying the seat forwards. Of course, when the horse is in forward motion, his centre of gravity is also moving forwards, so if the rider just sits like an inanimate object, e.g. a sack of potatoes, without a sense of going forward, he falls behind the movement and becomes a burden to the horse.

▶ To learn to be relaxed, it is important to have a trustworthy horse and be in a safe situation, so that you can let go of tensions and sit by balance alone. As your balance improves it may feel as though you aren't really riding anymore, just 'being there' ...

this is the real thing

▶ The quieter a rider you become, the more your body can listen to the horse's body, and give appropriate aids. Whenever your body is tensed to stay with the horse, it cannot be receptive enough to receive the constant flow of physical messages from the horse.

Looking ahead, 'feel' and balance

To achieve a sense of balance on horseback you need to look ahead. Human heads are heavy. They are also precariously placed on top of the neck. It is important that we balance this heavy piece of thinking gear nicely over our bodies, otherwise all kinds of tension creep in.

> Not only is the head heavy, I also believe that, when riding, even the human eyeballs can weigh around twenty stone! What I mean by this is that when the rider looks down, even with just their eyes, it seems to have the effect of putting the horse more on the forehand. This is particularly so in canter. During canter the horse has to lift his inside shoulder with each stride, but if the rider is weighting the shoulder with twenty stones of unnecessary eyeball, it becomes far more difficult for the horse to give his best!

Looking down

1. One of the most common reasons for looking down is to keep checking whether the horse is 'on the bit' or not. If you look ahead rather than down, you will start to 'feel' not only when the horse's head is correct, but also and

> When you find true balance, you will feel in a space of stillness; you let go of muscle tension in your body and legs.

more importantly, when his body is in a good shape. When the eyes are taking in a broad picture by looking ahead, the brain receives massively more information from the body through feel. I cannot emphasise this enough, and I know that looking down is a damned hard habit to eradicate.

2. I have a theory about riders who look down so much: they are unconsciously checking whether the place they expect to land if they fall off is soft or not. Their survival instinct is looking for any jagged rocks or prickly cacti that may be there. (The more you look down to check out suitable places to hit the deck, the more likely your focus and disturbed balance are to help you actually experience hitting the deck!)

3. Our centre of balance is in our inner ear, so it stands to reason that if the head, and therefore the inner ear, is tilted, our balance is going to be detrimentally affected.

4. Many people tend to look down when they are thinking. Engaging in thought whilst riding is fine, but the tendency to drop the head forwards, or sideways, like Rodin's thinker, is far from ideal.

The looking-ahead trick

Pick a post, school letter or tree in the distance, and ride to it whilst keeping your eyes on it.

See if you can count to a hundred while you ride, without looking down. Go back to one every time you look down; it's not easy, but the horse will probably go much better.

Horses often find ways to distract you from looking where you want to go; the more inclined you feel to look down or at the horse, the more you need to look ahead. Horses will trip up, stop for a scratch, speed up, slow down, go crooked, shy – in fact a whole host of things in order to get you off your direction – but the more unshakable you are, the less they will do it.

Remembering to breathe!

It's amazing how difficult things can become if you forget to breathe: even living gets tricky in a very short space of time. It is also amazing how much one can stop breathing deeply and freely whilst riding, either through concentration or anxiety. I have one friend who is a very experienced rider, but could only canter round the school twice without feeling weak and ill; we then realised that she held her breath whilst cantering!

Breathing into all of your rib cage helps to put you into a good upright

Great riding is made up of thousands of tiny details – that's all!

position and brings vital energy to all parts of the body. Points to look for are:

1. Try breathing quite slowly. Remember, when we are anxious our breathing speeds up. Horses are the same, and they notice if your breathing speeds up. Breathing slowly can help your thoughts to flow more easily too.

2. When you breathe in, try to do it so that your bottom rib moves outwards slightly.

3. Imagine breathing into the underside of your armpits or even into your seat, thighs or buttocks.

4. Be sure you breathe down into your lungs, and NOT up into your shoulders. Shoulders should not really get involved at all in breathing. If they do, then the contact on the reins can become less supple.

5. Don't overdo it, or you'll hyperventilate and pass out.

6. As you breathe, experiment with allowing your lower jaw and lips to relax. This can have a mirrored effect on a tight-mouthed horse, helping him to relax his jaw too.

The breathing trick

Here is a visualisation exercise to get any part of your body to relax. Let's say you want to relax your seat, for example: as you breathe in imagine doing so through your hands, then as you breathe out, imagine breathing out through your seat. Do this a few times and you will find that your seat has relaxed. Other areas to 'breathe out' may be your lower back, shoulders, upper thighs, neck, the top of the head, or underneath your heels.

'Mirror, mirror, on the hoof...'

One of the things that strikes me more and more, and most particularly with relation to the riding position, is how much horses mirror their riders. See a great rider on a horse, and the horse looks like a million dollars: see a plebeian on the same horse, and you don't even recognise it as the same animal.

When the rider sits with balance, poise and suppleness, the horse is almost compelled to reflect the same qualities. If the rider sits with stiffness, it becomes physically impossible for the horse to flow underneath. If the rider sits out of balance and 'all-to-cock', the horse cannot compensate for both the rider and himself (although some make a saintly and noble job of trying).

If you feel the horse resisting, instead of assuming that the fault is instigated by the horse, firstly try taking responsibility yourself. Check where you are stiff, out of balance, holding on, or not released and flowing. Nine times out of ten, working on your own body improves something in the horse: e.g. if your lower back is hollow and stiffened, probably the horse will be the same; if you poke your nose, the horse will happily poke his; if you don't give yourself freely to the movement, the horse will not be able to move freely. If you sit softly and in balance, the horse will have a great chance of going like a dream.

Soft, soft, *soft*, *soft*

> Feel the 'pads' of your seat as the intimate connection points between you and the horse.

Imagine being a horse and having someone sitting on your back. How would you like them to sit, hard or soft? Let me guess.

Would you like someone to 'push you on' with a 'driving' seat? Let me guess.

Create an inviting space into which the horse would want to bring up his back, by sitting softly. This is the most harmonious way to get him to work properly. Tensing your buttock or stomach muscles, pushing downwards into the saddle, or driving the horse forward with the seat only serve to make the horse less willing to round softly and swing his back freely; the rider then has to use stronger legs, seat and hands to get a result. The less force and the more 'invitation' you can use to shape the horse, the more splendid the outcome. Although it is important to sit correctly and with poise, think of being soft inside your body, from head to toe.

To do this well is no easy task, but this applies to most worthwhile aspects of riding.

> ONLY WHEN THE SEAT IS SOFT AND QUIET IS IT POSSIBLE FOR THE RIDER TO HEAR (FEEL) THE WHISPERS FROM THE HORSE. ONLY THEN CAN THE RIDER ASK THE RIGHT THING, IN THE RIGHT WAY, AT THE RIGHT TIME.

Common ways to sit imperfectly

As I said at the beginning of this chapter, there are lots of books that tell you how you should sit, but here we shall look at ways not to sit and how to correct them. This list of faults may seem daunting, but perfection in riding only exists as that slightly-out-of-reach goal, that holy grail to which we are all reaching out, and which we only seem to glimpse for moments. Earnest practice at improving your seat will mean that the divine moments become more frequent and easier to repeat. I hope the guidelines below help you to achieve those glimpses a little more often.

1. CHAIR SEAT: This is where the rider's feet are too far forward and not directly underneath his hips. This position puts the rider behind the horse's centre of gravity, leaves him behind the forward momentum of the horse, and makes all the leg, hand and seat aids much less effective. In this position the rider becomes a burden, and a hindrance to the horse's ability to move.

Possible solutions: It is often the case that rather than the feet being too far forward, the rider's seat is actually too far back. Try standing up in the stirrups so that your seat is up over the pommel, without knee-grip and without holding yourself up there with the reins or leaning on the horse's neck. Just get well forward with the hips, use balance and pray a lot. Now you've come forward and your legs are in the right place underneath your seat, very slowly slide lightly down the pommel and back into the saddle, leaving your feet where they were when you were standing up in the stirrups. Now stand up and do it again, because a few seconds after getting back in the saddle, you will probably have pressed your feet down too hard onto the stirrups, and pushed your seat back to where it started from (more on this in Chapter 4). Stroke the horse's neck for putting up with this stuff.

If your seat is already in the front of the saddle, you may need to lose the chair seat by bending the knees until the feet are further back and therefore underneath you – but this also requires an equal amount of bend in the ankles, which can be difficult to do softly. This can be made easier by having longer stirrups, or not wearing long, restricting riding boots.

As the joints, muscles and tendons at the tops of your legs become freer and easier to release, it will gradually become easier to have your legs hanging wherever you wish. **This is a gradual process and should not be attempted with force.**

> **THINK OF SITTING IN THE FRONT PART OF THE SADDLE. PUT AS LITTLE PRESSURE AS POSSIBLE ON THE STIRRUPS.**

2. STIFFNESS: This is very common in adult riders. Having stiff hips or shoulders, or a stiff back, etc. are problems that are with us most of the time, and come about as a result of that all-too-hazardous pastime called 'living', but they tend to become more noticeable when riding. At risk of litigation, during my years of coaching riders I have found accountants and lawyers to be at the

Ask yourself: 'Am I listening to the horse's body with my body, right now, and always?'

top of the league in the stiffness stakes!

Much stiffness comes about from being out of vertical balance with ourselves, then having to do lots of gravity-defying contortions in order not to fall off.

Let me explain: if, for example, you carry your head too far forward, you have to hold your shoulders too far back as a counter-weight, which in turn means you may carry your hips too far forwards as a counterweight to your shoulders. We humans will make quite a bit of effort in order not to fall over (when sober). The stiffness comes as a result of having constantly to use lots of muscles to hold these various parts of the body in defiance of gravity. So instead of trying to unstiffen this or that, which are the symptoms, let's firstly work on the problem, which is vertical balance.

Possible solution: Sit sideways-on to a full-length mirror, and align your shoulders over your hips. Contrary to riding teachers shouting, 'Shoulders back, **SHOULDERS BACK**!' you may even have to bring your shoulders forwards a little to place them over your hips. This will probably feel wrong, as you may feel like falling forwards. Don't panic –it's because your head is too far forward. Instead of pushing your head back, touch the tops of your ears with your fingers, then the end of your nose (so that you know the difference between ears and nose!) Now just **THINK** of the tops of your ears going up, and not your nose.

Now place the back of one hand in the small of your back, and allow your stomach to relax and your lower back to breathe out gently against your hand: this will let you lower your seat. Now place a hand on your sternum (breastbone), and allow that to soften slightly under your hand. If you were sitting on a saddle you would now be sitting deeper and more in balance, and much of the stiffness would have magically disappeared. You may now feel as though you are slumping. Get someone you trust to tell you if you are, or trust the mirror, rather than the unfamiliar feelings you are experiencing.

> THINK OF YOUR BODY ABOVE THE WAIST FLOATING UP, AND EVERYTHING BELOW THE WAIST LETTING GO AND DROPPING DOWN.

3. SITTING LOP-SIDED AND/OR TWISTED: Every human and every horse is one-sided to some degree or other. One-sidedness in the rider can have a major effect on the horse's ability to perform properly, especially when doing school-work. Most of us carry our hips slightly more to one side of the saddle than the other, as a result of which we carry our shoulders slightly over in the opposite way as a counterweight.

Many of us are also twisted (physically, at least!), and have one side of the body (hip and shoulder) ahead of the other, which definitely affects the ability to turn the horse evenly both ways, as well as interfering with superb canter work. It is interesting to note that out of all the times I've fallen off a horse, every single time except twice has been to the left (once to the right and once clean off the back). Naturally, since weight aids are so essential it is important not to sit one-sided; it may also help the rider to stay on board more (always a good thing).

Possible solutions: Firstly you need to find out to which side your hips slide across the saddle. It can be hard to feel this at first, because we spend twenty-four hours a day like it, so get someone with a good eye to tell you. Or, trot or canter both ways round on a 20m circle bareback, or at least with no stirrups, and feel when your hips start sliding to the outside; notice also any tendency to lean your shoulders into the circle like a motorbike.

So if your hips slide, say, over to the right when going round to the left, what you need to do is think of stepping down a stair with your left foot. This should bring your hips more over to the centre, and will open up the left ribs, which until now were squashed up. Now think of the tops of your ears (NOT YOUR NOSE!) going up to the sky. Now do all that again, because at first your body will slip back to its normal (habitual) place almost immediately. As you make these adjustments when riding a circle, the horse should start to take on a better shape, giving you confirmation that you are more evenly lined-up.

To deal with one side of your body being behind the other, ride a 20m circle with someone standing exactly in the middle. Ask them to tell you if they can see more of your outside shoulder blade, in which case you need to bring your outside forward a bit; alternatively if they can see more of your outside breast, you need to bring your outside back a little. It is usual always to have the same twist, so once you get to know which is your habit, you can remind yourself. This should particularly help in getting canter transitions equally good each way.

4. FORK SEAT: This is almost the opposite of the chair seat. Here the rider sits too much on the crotch, and not enough on the actual seat bones and buttocks. This position can cause the lower back to be too hollow, and therefore not mobile enough to move well with the horse. Riders who try too hard to get their legs back can end up sitting on their fork.

The disadvantages of sitting on the fork, as well as being less able to flow with the horse's back, are that the rider's crotch is not such a comfortable pad on the horse's back as is the seat, and there is less security for the rider.

Possible solutions: On a trustworthy horse, place your whole leg up in front of the saddle flap, so as to be sitting in a chair! From this position you should

It remains a mystery to me how it is possible for men to ride at all without doing themselves a mischief, and from this point of view, the fork seat should bring tears to the eyes. Strangely it doesn't: I managed to ride with a fork seat for some considerable time in the past and am still completely operational, as far as I know.

be able to fully feel your seat bones on the saddle. This position will also help to 'de-hollow' the small of the back. To further assist the softening your lower back, rest a hand there for a while so you can feel it, and then allow the vertebrae to release themselves into your hand.

The challenge now is to let the legs hang back down below the hips, without the pelvis tilting you back onto the crotch again. Having more bend in the knee, so that the feet are below the hips, is a sound move, until the hips develop enough flexibility and 'release' to get the legs back and the seat remaining on the saddle. Nothing here is achieved by force, it takes time and an unimaginable amount of toned relaxation and flexibility.

> REMEMBER: NO EFFORT … JUST LOADS OF DOING LESS THAN NOTHING!

5. THE 'QUASIMODO' AND EMBRYONIC SEATS: These are pretty obvious. The former is where the rider hunches his shoulders and bends the spine forwards. This position gives poor balance and makes the rein aids far less effective. Unfortunately, many teachers try to correct this fault by saying, 'Shoulders back, shoulders back, sit up straight, sit up straight.' Whilst these instructions aren't exactly wrong, they tend to lead riders to end up sitting too stiffly, with pinned-back shoulders.

The embryo seat is often the product of the human's natural reaction to protect their vital parts by curling up. Some of the causes of this seat are down to mental patterns of fear, anxiety, etc., but one of the key features of riding well is the need to overcome our natural reactions. The fact is: the more you can sit in vertical balance, the safer it is to ride. Curling up makes you very ineffective in terms of controlling the horse or your body.

Possible solutions: A way to cure crouching or bending forwards is to touch the top of your ears, then your nose, so that you know for sure which is which. Now think of your ears going upwards: this will help to take you up in a more natural way. Remember to try always to look ahead and not down, as this will help keep you naturally straight and up. (Read Chapter 14, on confidence and nerves.)

6. SERGEANT-MAJOR POSITION: This is quite commonly seen in those riders who try too hard, and often in the competition dressage arena, but not often by the very best dressage riders (e.g. Reiner Klimke). Here the shoulders are held too far back and the lower back is too hollow and stiff. This position doesn't permit the seat to flow enough with the horse's back nor allow the hands to

> Think about how good you look on that horse!

flow with the horse's mouth. It is quite difficult to breathe deeply and naturally in this position, which doesn't help performance either. The funny thing about this position is that it often looks really good to spectators.

Possible solutions: Quit riding with that poker up your a***! Place a hand on your sternum so that you can feel it. Now imagine the sternum is a hinge that can open and close the chest. Allow the hinge to close a little. Stand sideways-on to a full-length mirror and see if your shoulders are above your hips or behind them: they should be above. If you're used to riding with S and M shoulders (sergeant-major, not sado-masochist), closing the sternum a little may feel like you now have rounded shoulders and a slump; you may even get paranoid that you now look like one of those beginners who ride in the embryo position. Don't worry. See what effect it has on the horses, particularly on their carriage and softness in the mouth.

The second step is to place a hand on the small of your back, and allow that to relax also.

7. HEAD-BOBBERS: It is not uncommon to see excessive bobbing of the head, arms, hands or shoulders. The motion of the horse produces a wave of movement, which has to be absorbed by the rider somewhere. If this motion isn't absorbed adequately in the waist and lower back, it comes out somewhere else, including via the rider's head.

Possible solution: Learning to give and release in the lower back and stomach, and relaxing the waist and seat will cure the bouncing or bobbing (see sections above on how to do this).

8. 'LADY HAUGHTY OF ROYAL TONBRIDGE WELLS': This is another manifestation of trying too hard. Whilst it is important to look ahead and maintain a degree of 'carriage' when riding, poking the nose in the air is not ideal. What poking the nose in the air does, is cause tension through the rider's neck and back.

Possible solution: If the nose-poking rider drops the nose a little, often the horse will immediately do the same, as if parodying his human counterpart.

Imagine you're a horse...

You have a noble disposition, and try to give the best you can (mostly).

Things to do...

1. Take a series of lessons in the Alexander technique. This will improve your riding whilst off the horse.

2. Take as many lessons on the lunge as you can get. There is no substitute for the luxury of being able to concentrate solely on your riding, without having to think about guiding the horse.

3. Experiment with changes to your posture whilst riding a familiar horse, and see how it affects the horse. Try copying great riders by careful study of photographs, and see what effect it has on the horses when you pretend to ride like a maestro.

4. Stand on one leg, with your hands in the rein position, and look down at your feet. Now get a friend to push you over. 'BUMP', over you go! Now do exactly the same thing again, but this time look straight ahead: you will be much more solid and balanced.

5. Try out the POSSIBLE SOLUTIONS sections earlier in this chapter.

6. Get someone to video you riding in walk, trot and canter: watching 30 seconds of it should teach you a mountain of stuff about your riding and what you need to work on.

7. Think of the horse's back being your back, and think of softening and releasing, softening and releasing inside, WITHOUT slumping, or being too bendy or floppy. Sit on the horse in a way that you would find acceptable if you were a horse.

Quick reference...

Ears over shoulders, shoulders over hips, hips over feet; try to 'feel' your point of balance; stand up with bent knees and a horse between your legs; breathe; everything below the waist drops down; the head floats up; time learning a good seat is never wasted; try the Alexander technique; look ahead; have poise, but be soft, soft, soft; horses are mirrors, they reflect how to sit and how not to sit.

Legs, legs, legs!

There is a lot written and said about 'legs' in riding: e.g. use lots of leg; ride him off the leg; get him in front of the leg; keep your leg on; leg him on; you need good strong legs, etc. It is true to say that the legs are a key element in effective riding for a number of reasons, but where should your legs be and how are the legs best used?

Where should the legs be?

Ideally, the rider's legs should be in a position so that the rider's feet are under his seat. That means that if the stirrups are short, the rider needs quite a lot of bend in the knee, hip and ankle joints, so that the feet don't come forwards; and if the stirrups are long, all those joints can be straighter. Either way, for optimum balance and effectiveness, the feet should be under the rider's seat

Often riders try to 'get their legs back', but this isn't always ideal: yes, the legs may need to be further back – but by being allowed to be so by releasing more and more in the hip joints, rather than by forced stretching. There is a common tendency to sit with the seat too far back in the saddle instead of in the 'front' of the saddle: this fault often means that the feet are in front of the seat, but not because the legs need to go back, but because the seat needs to come forwards.

Try standing up in the saddle, at which point your feet will be in the right place below your seat. Now slide your seat down into the front of the saddle, without your feet going anywhere! Not easy, hey?

> **Allow the weight of the leg to drop down naturally (legs are quite heavy).**

If I could offer you one piece of advice about how the legs should feel, it would be '**let your legs fall away from your body at the hips**'. If the legs are held in place, they become stiff and hard to move and the hips become locked, which means the rider cannot flow with the horse's movement and the legs also become unable to 'listen' to the horse. Wow!

Ideally, the more the legs can be allowed to 'fall away' from the rider's body, the better. That does not mean that the lower leg should stick out away from the horse; in fact, if the top of the rider's leg falls away from the body, the lower leg will naturally find a nice, gentle contact with the horse's sides.

Want some imagery for this? In place of your legs, imagine you have pinned a three-foot long dead cod fish onto each side of your pelvis. How would they hang down against the horse's sides? That's about right!

Feet, ankles and stirrups

Ask youself: 'How much weight, in pounds, ounces or kilograms, do I have on the stirrups right now?' See if you can lighten the weight on the stirrups and at the same time have a longer, deeper heel.

Have a soft ankle joint. The ankle joint absorbs much of the horse's movement, believe it or not.

If the feet are forced to face too much to the front this causes tension in the ankle and knee joints. Release those joints slightly so that the position of the feet becomes more natural.

If the feet poke outwards too much it makes you grip more with the calves, which means you are not riding with balance. This will make lazy horses go slower, and fast horses take off with you! Not ideal. To help with this, think of the lower back being softer and the back of the buttocks being allowed to be wider apart! This will release the whole leg so that the feet will eventually lie more naturally to the front. Find a way to motivate the horse with **much** lighter leg aids, to help you release the legs.

Have a very light contact with the stirrup. If any more than a light pressure is applied to the stirrup, it actually pushes your seat up off the saddle!

Try this: Sit on a bar stool (whilst still fairly sober), and rest your feet naturally on the foot-rests – the pressure will be very light. Now press down onto the foot-rests and feel your bottom start to leave the seat of the stool. Stirrups are not part of a safety kit; they are just somewhere to rest your feet lightly. (I must confess, though, that having stirrups has helped me stay on once or twice!)

There is lots of talk about riding without stirrups. This is great provided it doesn't lead to you gripping with your legs to stay on in trot and canter, in which case it's best not to bother: learning to ride by balance takes time, but it won't happen if you are gripping with the calves or thighs. Once the stirrups are re-introduced some of the benefits of a deeper seat from riding with no stirrups are lost unless the ankles are soft enough.

Knees

A common source of confusion is this question: '**I used to be taught the old way of gripping with my knees, but isn't the new way of riding not to grip?'**

Actually, gripping with the knees was never really the 'old' way, nor is it the best way to ride for lots of reasons. My best guess is that being told to grip with the knees came about around the time of the Caprilli seat, just over a hundred years ago, as a quick-fix way of teaching non-riding infantry squaddies to ride a horse well enough in a few weeks to go off to war and be cannon fodder. Prior to that, riding was taught in the true classical way, with balance and poise – and it takes lots of time to learn. The so-called new way of not gripping with the knees is simply going back to the correct method of riding as practised for thousands of years.

A seriously questionable practice, which I gather is being taught even in some British riding instructors' colleges, is to purposely have a gap between the rider's knee and the saddle. This is surely an over-correction from the mistake of years of teaching people to grip, but I believe it is quite incorrect and unsafe. If your teacher is teaching you this way, don't hang around to argue the point, just go and find a different teacher. In an extensive library of equestrian literature written by masters from 500 BC to the present day, I have yet to find anyone saying that it is correct to have a gap between your knee and the saddle.

If you allow the legs to fall away from your body, the knees should lie naturally on the saddle, without grip or a gap.

Imagine you're a horse...

You have a definite sense of your own body-space.

Thighs

The thighs need to be very soft and not gripping, especially on the inside at the top where they join your groin area. This looseness allows the horse's back and ribs to expand and his body to flow. It also helps you to absorb more of the horse's movement and to ride with balance. Developing an awareness of just how relaxed and soft the thighs need to be is quite a task. It takes time to feel totally released through the thighs.

What are the purposes of the legs?

1. Impulsion/forwardness

The rider's legs ask the horse to move forwards or ask for more energy from the horse's hindquarters. If the aid is accurately timed (see the chapters on the aids, and the three paces) the leg aid has the most effect.

It is best not to keep asking all the time with the legs, as this will make the horse less responsive and the rider tired. Instead, ask for what you want, get it and let the legs lie quietly against the horse until the next time you have to ask.

Leg aids can be so light as to be a breath against the horse's flanks, yet still get a reaction. If you find the need to give 'strong' leg aids, use a schooling stick to tune the horse up to lighter leg aid. Often, with an unresponsive type of horse, the stronger you use your legs, the less effort they will put in.

Try this: A good way to experience light legs is to hold your hands quite lightly on either side of a friend's ribs (better be quite a good friend!) and get them to trot on the spot. Now as they do this tickle them up lightly with your hands, ideally as they are going upwards: they will trot more actively.

Now do the same thing but hold their ribs quite firmly with your hands while they trot on the spot again, and as they go up each time squeeze their ribs even tighter: I bet they can hardly get off the ground!

Now relate that to horses: your hands are in the same place on your friend's ribs as your legs would be on a horse, and you can clearly see what happens.

2. Supporting the steering

With the turn of the rider's body, the legs should naturally follow suit. Generally speaking, on turns it is normal to have the inside leg on the girth (around which the horse steps as though the leg were a pillar) and the outside leg slightly further back. This outside leg position offers a passive way of supporting the turn and assisting the horse's back end to follow the line of the turn, instead of swinging outwards like the back end of a boat.

When turning, a good thought for the inside leg is to think of taking a step down a stair with that inside foot.

3. Stopping

This is a difficult thing to understand, since the main use of the legs is to make the horse go forwards. So how can the legs also be used to make the horse stop? Surprisingly the rider's legs can be used to withhold the horse's movement (as in highly collected work). As the rider asks for halt, the horse should feel that it is sent into passively resisting reins, which it meets and then stops. To do this means bringing the legs into slightly closer contact. Within the halt, the legs should soften slightly but remain in light contact with the horse; this maintains the horse's attention and means there is still energy in the halt: when you stop the car at traffic lights, you don't switch off the engine!

4. Framing/balance

The rider's legs naturally embrace the horse and have a greater area in contact with the horse than any other part of the rider's body. By subtly 'being there', and by quietly asking the horse to step from behind, the legs play a big part in keeping the horse balanced under the rider's weight. If the legs come away from the horse's sides, the horse may well fall out of balance in much the same way that a car becomes less 'contained' when the clutch is not engaged. With training (see poll-softening exercise in Chapter 18, To be or not to be 'on the bit') the horse learns to be softer on the bridle by the feel of the rider's legs.

As the horse becomes more balanced, nicely framed by the legs and responsive to gentle leg aids, you should find that he becomes softer in the mouth.

5. Details/lateral work

There are endless subtle messages that can be sent to the horse from the rider with the use of the legs. If the rider thinks about his precise intentions before giving the leg aids, the horse will often pick up on the meaning of the leg aid and respond accordingly. For example, an aid with the inside leg on the girth can say to the horse 'come around here' onto a circle, or it can say 'step over

Ask yourself: 'Who's doing all the work here? Me or the horse?'

into shoulder-in'.

Likewise, the rider's legs can think about having 5,000 volts going down them to get some real action, or they can be gently reassuring the horse and saying 'Calm down. Everything's OK'. It is mostly about the thought or intention behind the action.

With practice it becomes possible to ask the horse to move a specific foot by sending that thought down through the rider's legs ... now that is fine detail.

6. Being there / reminding the horse he's not alone

Having the legs gently on the horse's sides helps him to feel your presence. Sometimes this is really important, since without your presence and support, the horse is more likely to react first and think later in scary situations. The legs 'being there' can say to the horse 'It's OK. I'm with you. This is a safe place to be'.

7. Rider stability

Although we have seen that it is important to ride with balance and not by gripping with the legs, just by virtue of the fact that the legs are hanging in close contact with the horse's flanks, they give a degree of stability to the rider's position.

8. Listening legs

As we have seen, the legs can send a variety of subtle messages to the horse. If the legs are quiet and soft enough, they can also be used as receptors of subtle messages back from the horse. The legs can feel where the horse is stiff or soft, where his feet are at any given moment, what his rhythm is like, whether he is relaxed in his movement, his ribs and his mind, etc. This can only happen if the rider's legs are as quiet as possible.

Try reading out loud from a book whilst the radio is on: it is impossible to know what is being said on the radio because you are talking aloud yourself. It is the same with riding, and particularly with the legs. If the legs are doing 'stuff' all the time instead of being quiet, they cannot hear the whispers from the horse.

Imagine you're a horse...

You have a hectic social life, preferably twenty-four hours a day.

Common pitfalls

1. Using legs too much / all the time.

2. Not using legs and just relying on the reins for steering and stopping.

3. Gripping!

4. Having the seat too far back.

5. Too much pressure on the stirrup / heels pushed down too hard.

6. Trying too hard.

7. Kicking! An absolutely unhorsemanlike habit.

8. Not supporting the leg aids with a stick when needed.

9. Legs being pushed too far forwards.

10. Heels raised instead of hanging softly.

11. Legs just giving the same signal all the time instead of expressing thoughts.

12. Legs not listening to the horse.

Things to do...

1. Stand with your feet hip-width apart (about a foot), sideways-on to a full-length mirror. Hold your hands as though you have reins and bend your knees until you are in a riding position. Check in the mirror how your feet are underneath your seat and get a feel of it: if they aren't you'll probably fall over! Now simply take up the same position on the horse.

2. Check that you have a very light pressure on the stirrups by gently raising the FRONT of your feet.

3. Let your legs hang from your hips. Picture dead cod pinned onto your hips instead of legs!

4. See how much you can get the horse to do whilst keeping the leg aids to a minimum. Then try doing even less.

5. Stand up in the stirrups and then, when you sit down again, make sure you are in the deepest (near the front) part of the saddle.

Quick reference...

Legs are important; they can be used too much or too little; the feet should be under the seat; avoid gripping, let them be as relaxed as possible; the legs have many functions in riding; have a light pressure on the stirrups or you will push your seat out of the saddle.

Hand, fist, elbow and wrist

We *Homo sapiens* do just about everything with our hands; that's one of the key things that sets us apart from the other species that share the planet, including horses. Okay, so bears use their claws to poke honey out of beehives, some baboons use stones to crack open nuts, gorïllas use their forefinger to pick their noses, and chimpanzees play with themselves to entertain schoolboys visiting the zoo, but only humans have achieved global domination by virtue of having an 'opposing thumb'!

What we do with our hands when we ride is therefore pretty central to our way of thinking. We can get quite upset if people criticise the way we use our hands when we ride. Phrases like 'you have bad hands' or 'your hands are moving too much', or 'you're heavy-handed' are guaranteed to hit a nerve. In many ways it would be easier to learn to ride without having hands, since our desire to use them presents us with many pitfalls on the road to being a great rider.

In reality it is best to do as little as possible with the hands when you ride – and then when you can do that, do even less with them! Watch great riders

Imagine you're a horse...

You love galloping and doing spectacular things with your body; you love to pose.

and you will find it hard to see them doing much, if anything at all, with their hands. The hands act as subtle filters through which the horse's energy is channelled and directed.

'Bad hands' and 'good hands'

Good hands are light, consistent, allowing, elastic, feeling, alive, still, passive, listening, responsive, coaxing and even thoughtful.

Bad hands are heavy, erratic, untrustworthy, harsh, bouncing, pulling back, stiff, dead, rigid, unresponsive, domineering and unsympathetic.

Like most aspects of riding, all things are connected, so to acquire good hands requires us to look at a wider picture than just the hands themselves.

What goes into having good hands?

> For the rider's hands to be still, kind and elastic, the horse's movement has to be absorbed through the rider's body.

1. If you wish to have sensitive and light communication with the horse you are starting out with a good chance of achieving good hands (see Chapter 6 on contact). If you are used to having a strong connection with the horse and don't really care that much about what your hands are like, then the horse will tend to be strong and insensitive in return. It may unfortunately be the case that some teachers have taught you to ride with a strong contact and not introduced you to more refined or harmonious possibilities. There are even some riders who actually like a horse to be 'strong', pulling and fighting to go (but they ain't ever riding any of my favourite horses, that's for sure).

2. When the horse is in motion there is quite a bit of movement from his body, which comes up through the rider's body and down the arms to the hands, especially in trot and canter. For the rider's hands to be still and elastic, it is therefore necessary for the rider's body to absorb the movement of the horse, so that by the time it gets to the hands they can be kept quiet and still in relation to the horse's mouth. This is done by developing a soft seat, ankles, legs, waist, chest, shoulders, neck and wrists – which I know sounds a tall order. Not everyone finds it easy, but it will come if approached with patience and time. The softer all of these joints are, the easier it is for the rider to have good hands.

3. The more correct the positioning of the hands, wrists, shoulders and elbows, the easier it is to develop a fine degree of communication with the horse

Think how strong a horse can be and how weak your wrists are … then straighten the wrists!

through the hands. (See below: 'Correct positioning and energy flow'.)

4. Less is more (again!).The less 'stuff' you try to make the horse do with your hands, the more effective you will become as a rider and the better your hands will be.

5. Start to believe that hands can listen, think and have different attitudes, regardless of what they appear to be doing physically. Now if that sounds pretty alien, let me give you some clues: without moving or appearing to do anything physically different, the hands can have a 'giving' attitude or a restricting attitude. The hands can be 'deaf' to the tiny feelings from the horse, or they can be receptive and picking up those feelings. The hands can be kind, smiling and friendly or they can be strict and frowning. The hands can have an attitude of being 'alive' or quite 'dead'. All this subliminal communication can go on between the hands and the horse

Correct positioning and energy flow

Notice that this section discusses 'correct positioning' and not 'the correct position'. The hand, elbow and wrist need to be alive, and to adapt and flow with the situation; 'the correct position' implies something much more fixed.

Correct positioning of the hand, wrist, fist and elbow is so essential because it helps the energy and communication to flow between the horse and rider with the least resistance. If these body parts are not deployed in the simplest and most straightforward way, the energy and flow is disturbed, the rider has to use stronger hand aids, horses will tend to pull more against the rider and, believe it or not, the rider becomes less secure in the saddle. I have pulled many-an-unsuspecting rider off their seat by tugging on the reins when the positioning of their hands, fist, elbow and wrist wasn't simple and straightforward: most are shocked at how easily they are dislodged and immediately choose to learn the simple, straightforward – and safe – option!

The reins. Pick up the reins in a slow and sensitive manner (unless the horse is heading for the hills, of course, in which case try something more desperate!). Closing the fingers and making a fist around the reins gives more stability to the connection with the horse's mouth. It is not done for extra strength.

The elbows should be allowed to hang loosely, almost heavily, so that they can swing freely back and forth with the movement of the horse's head. Ideally they are not held too far forwards or too far back, but should hang around under the shoulders where the least muscular effort is required. A good thought to have is that your heavy elbows are connected to your lower spine on a piece of elastic. The elbows should lie naturally against the ribs, not sticking out like frozen turkey wings or squeezed into the ribs as if you're trying to hide a bad case of BO! Develop the sensation that it is your elbows and not your hands that are connected to the horse's mouth through the reins.

The wrists. These are so important. Ideally the back of the wrists should be nearly straight, which means not curling them in towards the stomach, like monkey hands, nor out like a 'biblical figure beseeching the Lord God' in an Baroque oil-painting. If the wrists are straight they will be able to be soft inside, without being floppy or insipid. If evolution had wanted to develop the perfect rider, I suspect that he would have no wrists or hands whatsoever, just a very long forearm that reached the horse's mouth. Try as much as possible to ride without bending or using your wrists.

If the wrists are not straight and soft the horse tends to pull more against them, rather than connecting with the rider's back.

The fists. Many people ride with their fingers open because they want to have light hands, which is a notion of the highest order. What this does, though, is make the hands more inconsistent, and means that the rider becomes stiffer somewhere else. If the fingers are closed, the hands become more consistent, so the horse knows more where he is. Also, the rider with a closed fist tends to be softer elsewhere, such as in the shoulders.

Check that your **thumbs** are relaxed too: if your thumbs are sticking up or tense they carry the tension to the wrists. The horse can even feel a stiff thumb – wow!

Instead of just closing the fingers, think of the outside of the hand stretching around until the fingers touch the palms. This gives the whole thing less of a grasping feel about it. Away from the horse, practise making a fist without the wrist getting tight.

It goes without saying that holding the fist closed, as though you are on a white-knuckle roller coaster ride or holding onto your last £20 note, is not ideal either: the fingers need to be closed gently.

The hands. By now you will understand that the hands themselves are but a small part of the whole. Even though people tend to talk about 'hands', what they are really referring to is the whole collection of body-parts from the seat, back, shoulders and elbows to the wrists and even the fingers.

The most effective place to have the hands is so that they form straight lines, both vertically and horizontally, between the horse's mouth and the rider's elbows. If the hands are held too high, too low, too near to each other or too far apart, then the same things happen as when the rider's wrists are not straight, basically things start getting unnecessarily complicated. As a result, the flow of energy between the rider and the horse is disrupted, the horse is more likely to get 'strong' and the rider is actually less secure in the saddle.

The simpler things are, the better – which means that if the horse's head is low then the rider's hands will need to follow by being lower, and if the horse's head is high, the hands will need to follow by going higher. It is common practice to see riders holding their hands low down on the horse's shoulders to 'try' and get his head down. This is not a terribly effective approach as it breaks the straight line of communication. This approach may have the effect of getting the horse's head down, but it does not engage the horse's back or hindquarters at all – basically, it is fools' gold.

Ideally the rider does nothing really active with the hands at all; they are 'just there', offering a consistent connection and communication with the horse, nothing much else. Sometimes things are not going ideally well and/or safety is jeopardised, in which case one has to do more, but this should be left as a last resort.

> Think of the hands as part of a two-way, subtle communication system, rather than a means of 'contol'.

The purposes of hands

Hands are used in conjunction with other aids to communicate with the horse. Let's look at what the special purposes of the hands are, and how they can best be applied.

Stopping: non-riders all know that to stop a horse you pull the reins! But what many riders know is that pulling on both reins doesn't necessarily stop a horse at all, and in some cases can even cause the horse to speed up!

The hands are indeed a part of stopping, slowing or re-balancing the horse, but only when used together with the mind, seat and legs of the rider. (Look at Chapter 8, 'Go, stop and changing gear' for more on this, especially about using the elbows rather than the hands.)

Steering: There are lots of different ways to steer horses. Pulling the rein on the same side as you wish to go (the inside rein) is just about the most incorrect way of doing it, albeit the most commonly used way.

'I want to go right, so I'm pulling the right rein and this ignorant horse is just going left with his head bent the wrong way!'

Ideally you steer the horse with both reins together, along with your mind and entire body, from your toes to your head. (See Chapter 9, 'Effective steering'.)

> Make sure your thumbs are on top – it helps the horse to collect more easily, makes the contact softer, and improves the flow of energy between you and the horse. Worth doing, huh?

Collection: This is a subject all to itself, but suffice to say here that collection or getting the horse on the bit is **partly** brought about by the presence of the hands. Emphasis here is on the word 'partly', because many other elements go along with the hands in collecting a horse correctly. Having a strong contact, whoever may have misled you into thinking otherwise, does not necessarily bring about collection. In fact, in many cases a strong contact can hinder the horse's ability to collect properly.

Things to do...

1. Get a friend to hold one end of a pair of reins (you can improvise with a light rope or something similar). Stand facing each other. One of you holds the 'reins' in the normal riding position, and one of you is the horse, holding both reins in one hand. The 'horse' moves the reins gently back and forth like a horse's head when walking. The 'rider' passively follows the movement. Make sure the 'horse' is the one initiating the movement. Make sure that the 'rider' is following the 'horse' with an even contact, so that weight never changes, and they are not just waving their hands back and forth. Also make sure you don't end up having a blazing row about who's pulling whom!

   This is a great exercise to help the rider learn to improve their passive, allowing, rein contact. If you play the part of the horse with more than one person, as I get people on my courses to do, you'll be amazed at how utterly different every rider feels: so much so, it's a wonder horses understand what we're on about at all!

2. Off the horse, practise letting your elbows hang from your shoulders and closing your fingers without tightening the wrists.

3. Start getting a feeling that your hands are sensitive, allowing the horse to go forward, and develop hands that actually listen to the horse.

4. Look for lightness between you and the horse. Experiment to see how light you can be and how the horse responds.

Quick reference...

Less is more; simple and correct positioning; think about being light and sensitive; use the hands as little as possible; remember that the hands are part of an ensemble, not used in isolation to give the aids.

Chapter 6

Contact – and the million-dollar question

Rein contact is the source of more confusion and difficulty than almost any other aspect of riding.

What is contact?

First, let's look at exactly what contact means in the dictionary and then try to demystify it.

1. The act or state of touching.

2. The state or fact of communication.

3. A junction of electrical conductors.

4. Any person who has been exposed to a contagious disease, etc.

Electrical junctions and contagious diseases aside, contact simply means 'communication through touch'. In the case of riding, it means communication between rider and horse, and horse and rider, by sending physical messages up and down the reins.

> Remember: the definition of contact is communication, not domination; and communication is a two-way thing.

What contact is not!

You may be surprised or relieved to hear that contact does not mean having the reins so short that your arms are being pulled off, that you feel more like an unlicensed equine dentist than a noble horseman, or that you get blisters on your fingers and your seat gets pulled forwards out of the saddle We have all been misled into experiencing these things at some time or other. Was it fun for us? No. Was it fun for the horse? Seems highly unlikely.

Is it vital to have a contact?

In a word ... sometimes!

The fact is that we don't **NEED** contact to ride, or even to get a horse to go well. People who always work their horses on a contact may say that riding with no contact is rubbish, just slopping along, not working properly, lazy, not 'proper' riding, just for cowboys, not a way to have adequate control, etc. At the end of the day, like many aspects of riding, it's down to personal taste, what your goals are with the horse and what you find pleasurable and fun. This is not to say we should all go out and become Western riders, just as it isn't true to say we must always have a constant contact.

Different approaches and amounts of contact bring different results: some approaches and results being more in harmony with the horse, and some approaches being more about domination (the horses you ride and your 'inner voice' should tell you which is which).

How much contact is correct?

One of the all-time million-dollar questions is. 'How much contact should I use?'

Unfortunately there is no simple answer and no absolute right or wrong. Like many aspects of riding, almost everyone will tell you something different, even many experts appear to disagree (damn!).

> This is what I always aim for: TO HAVE THE CONTACT AS LIGHT AS IT CAN BE, BUT AS FIRM AS IT HAS TO BE.

What does that mean?

> There is no 'right' or 'wrong' amount of contact: just be honest with yourself about how it feels to you and the horse in every moment.

'As light as it can be' is just enough weight so that you can feel the horse's mouth, he can feel your hands and the weight remains totally consistent – like a contract both of you are willing to sign.

'As firm as it has to be' means there may be moments when you need to emphasise your rein aids by having a firmer contact, as though you are pointing out to the horse that the contract includes a particular bit of small print that he may not have noticed!

Remember that the more firmly and more strongly you ride, the more firmly and more strongly you will have to ride. If you always aim for lightness with each new movement and each new moment, the horse should get lighter and lighter.

At the end of the day, there is nothing more pleasurable than a horse working well, whilst being totally light in the hand.

If you were a horse, how much contact would you like?

Some might say, 'What's that got to do with it? He's a big, strong animal and sometimes he pulls like a steam train. He doesn't act that sensitive.' If I were a horse I'd always want the contact to be light, comfortable and consistent. I think you'd agree.

The type of fleshy tissue in the horse's mouth is similar to our own, just larger. Our mouths, lips and tongues are quite sensitive (certainly feels like it when you're eating a hot Madras curry). It is a good idea to remember that the horse's mouth is capable of great sensitivity, despite the horse sometimes behaving otherwise.

Personal taste

Contact is a very personal thing for humans.

Teacher, trainer or judge Mr Holdemlight may like horses to go with 3 ounces of weight in the reins; and teacher, trainer or judge Mr Holdemtight may prefer 15lbs in the reins.

Here's the simple answer. When you ride with Mr Holdemlight have 3 ounces of contact, and when you ride with Mr Holdemtight have 15lbs: if you do that you'll probably be fine. Afterwards, you can decide which one you prefer. I know which one I prefer and which I'd prefer if I were a horse!

It is not a matter of whether Mr Holdemlight or Mr Holdemtight is right or wrong, it is just personal preference. Remain flexible: there is no hard-and-fast rule about contact. Even if you ride the same horse for two days running, you may need to use different amounts of contact. Even from one minute to the next you may need to use different amounts of contact. **Provided you seek to be light, consistent, and look for a harmonious 'feel' with the horse, you won't go far wrong.**

'Consistent' means that the contact has a steady and reliable quality – not limp then jerky, then hard, then wobbly, then oops! banged in the teeth, then like wet lettuce, then like a grip from Robo-Cop, then vague. It is about being trustworthy for the horse.

Too little / too much

On a scale of 1 to 10, how much fun are you having? Do what you can to get it up to at least 8, right now!

There will be times when you use too little contact: moments when we need to offer more than the minimum resistance (see passive resistance section below). Perhaps the horse is rushing a little too much, or needs rebalancing, or is falling in or out on a turn, or is disregarding more subtle aids, or is gazing off to one side or the other. It is also true to say that some horses feel more secure if they have a little more than the minimum contact – it helps sometimes to let them know you're there.

Try to make the firmer contact last for as little time as possible, even as little as the duration of one of the horse's strides or footfalls, then be light again. If you need to, repeat the firmer resistance again, and then be light again. Each time the horse gives the tiniest bit, instantly give a little and be lighter yourself.

There will be times when you use too much contact. Riding a horse on more contact than it can comfortably cope with brings about many difficulties. Rearing, bolting, pulling, bucking, napping, being slug-like, going too fast, too slow, jogging, getting tense, yanking the bit – all these things and more can be caused by having too much contact, to say nothing of the rider having a miserable time, with their arms, shoulders and back aching.

Riding on a contact is a real art; it can also be a minefield laden with difficulties.

Paradoxically, many horses will speed up rather than slow down as you tighten the reins. Some will run to get away from the discomfort in their mouths or the amount of contact which makes them feel claustrophobic, or the contact restricts their ability to move and balance properly, so they end up on the forehand and speed up to catch up with their own balance!

Opening the front door

Ask yourself: 'Is this the lightest contact I could have right now and still get the same result?'

A common aspect of using too much contact is not 'opening the front door' enough when asking the horse to go forwards. Many riders ask the horse to walk on, or go forwards, but the contact does not ease up enough, so the forward movement is actually blocked before it even starts.

Horses aren't dumb, so when the rider asks them to go forwards but doesn't open the front door, even a crack, the horse thinks, 'Well, you obviously don't really mean go forwards. You must be a confused human and don't really know what you want, so I'll just do nothing,' or if he's the sensitive type then maybe he'll go backwards or even rear. If the horse is very sensitive he may get anxious and start 'playing up' at this point. The front door doesn't need to be opened so wide that the removal men could carry in a grand piano, or that the reins hang down like builders' pants: it can be opened just wide enough to let the cat slip out or check it's not the bailiffs on the doorstep!

The thing that happens when the horse doesn't respond to the rider saying go forward through the solid wall of contact is that the rider thinks the horse isn't responding to the leg, at which point the horse is often then treated to a couple of kicks in the ribs and mutterings about how unwilling and damned lazy he is.

Even a slight give within the hand just before asking for forwardness may be enough, but with a really 'plugged-up' or confused horse, sometimes it's worth holding the reins right out in front of you for a few moments, even with your arms straight ahead, to make the request to go forwards abundantly clear. (Make sure you're looking ahead and not down at the horse too!)

Passive resistance vs active rein aids

Ask yourself: 'Are my hands being active or passive at this moment?'

The difference between 'active' and 'passive' rein aids is little more than a thought or an attitude. Since it is little more than a thought, at least you don't have to be a brilliant rider to have a go at this.

'**Active**' has an attitude of pulling back with the hands, actively restricting the horse. '**Passive**' can consist of just as firm a contact in the reins as 'active', but there is an attitude of the hand 'just being there'. All this may sound about as important as whether you wear pink or blue knickers on a Tuesday, but believe it or not, the difference of attitude in the hand makes the world of difference to horses.

Most horses will pull far less against 'passive' side-reins or a tie-ring on a wall than they will against a rider. The rider, on the other hand, is often actively trying to achieve some result, like making an ill-prepared turn, stop, 'get that

Accept that the horse is perfect, then keep progressing from there.

horse on the bit', or 'under control'.

To achieve passive resistance requires the rider to sit nicely upright, to have bent elbows, straight hands and wrists, a smile on his face, a calm mind and a relaxed jaw. Sit and wait for the horse to figure it out.

The difference in horses' responses to active and passive rein aids is amazing. If the rein aid is active, i.e. pulling back, horses seem to pull against it and find it disturbing. If the rein is passively resisting (remember the difference is mostly in the mind), horses seem to work it out for themselves without getting upset.

Riding with no contact

It is difficult, if not impossible, to develop an independent seat if the rider learns to ride always with a contact. We humans are very good at steadying ourselves and staying upright with help from our hands, including using the reins.

Without an independent seat our hands are not free to have a steady and consistent contact with the horse's mouth. Achieving an independent enough seat to have steady hands is not a quick, easy task, but if approached honestly, it is not beyond anyone to do it really well.

An excellent way to achieve this independence of hands and seat is to practise riding with no contact whatsoever, in walk, trot and canter – **SHRIEKS OF HORROR from all directions**, but – being on the lunge is a great and an accepted way to learn.

Take an attitude of 'showing' the horse what you want – explain to him in a way he can understand.

Another way is to practise riding on a totally loose rein, i**n a safe situation**, and learn to guide the horse by suggestion and body position. Turn your whole body the way you want to go; stop moving your seat bones to halt; move your seat bones to go forward; etc. Use your legs, long reins and common sense to reinforce your 'body suggestion' to the horse. If you learn to do this quite well, riding with a steady contact will be so much easier, more effective and more harmonious.

Contact in walk, trot and canter

The next important step towards effective riding with a contact is to be able to follow the horse's mouth in all three paces, so that the weight in the reins stays light and consistent.

▶ **IN WALK** the horse's head nods back and forth. See if you can **passively**

If riding was quick and easy to learn, it wouldn't be nearly so addictive.

follow that nod. Look ahead and let your arms swing passively back and forth freely from the shoulder.

▶ **IN TROT** the horse's head doesn't nod, it stays still relative to the riders' hands and the riders' body moves instead, e.g. in rising trot. This means that your arms still have to be able to pivot or swing from the shoulder, but in trot your body moves back and forth and your hands must remain still – now there's a challenge, eh?

▶ **IN CANTER** the horse's head again moves back and forth, and so, to some degree, does your body. Sounds difficult, but if you can do it in walk and trot, having a steady contact in canter should not create any new difficulties (we hope!).

Feel the rhythm

It is more difficult for the rider to keep a nice, even contact if the horse's rhythm is irregular or uneven. Pay attention to the rhythm and ride in a regular rhythm yourself, Choose the tempo (speed) you want to go, keep it ticking in your head, use your body, legs and lastly your hands to get the horse and yourself to stay in a regular, consistent rhythm. As the horse becomes more consistently rhythmical, it becomes much easier to keep an even contact.

Suppleness

Generally speaking, the more supple a horse is through his whole body, the lighter the contact you can have with him. If a horse is soft and flexible in all his joints and muscles, it stands to reason that he will be lighter in the mouth and better able to carry out his rider's wishes without having to be forced into an outline.

The need to be flexible creates enormous difficulties for riders who only ride the average riding-school horse. These most noble creatures are not normally the most supple in the world, and therefore don't always give the clear-

Imagine you're a horse...

You think you are always an item on Nature's menu: you believe you taste delicious.

est picture of how horses can feel, including the lightness of contact. Naturally if they were particularly light, riding school horses would either get upset with different riders, or create chaos by being too sensitive for people to cope with.

Vibrating ... with the reins

A little-talked-about trick which sometimes helps is to vibrate the reins. This is not in any way, shape or form jerking, tugging or see-sawing the reins from either side, which is unseemly, unhorsemanlike and unpleasant to behold. It is a secret and subtle vibrato, like that used on the fretboard of a violin. It is done quite rapidly, only ever with one hand at a time, and within the hand itself, so that no one can see it, even if the onlooker is right next to you.

> Make what you are doing **so** interesting that the horse wants to listen to you.

Some horses respond better than others to this vibration. Vibrate one rein just when you feel the horse start to ignore your communications or start leaning on one hand more than the other. **Stop vibrating the rein as soon as the horse responds.** Doing it all the time would be as ineffective as when one half of a married couple nags all the time, and the other half mostly ignores them (I daren't say any more about that).

Time out

Every few minutes or so, at a suitable moment, it is a good idea to ease off the contact and let the horse have a longer rein. This has a positive effect on the horse and rider, both physically and mentally. Grinding away on a contact can become just that, a grind. But if the horse gets a minute or two of time out 'on parole', when you pick up the contact again, it's like you are both starting afresh: new rider and new horse. It also gives the horse a chance to stretch his muscles.

Fun and pleasure

When you're riding on a contact, remind yourself of why you are riding – it's supposed to be for fun and pleasure, isn't it? Riding on a contact should be pleasurable, both for you and the horse.

Don't believe everything people tell you. In the end the only person who really knows the truth for you is **YOU**. If something doesn't feel right about riding on a contact for you, and your teacher's explanation isn't convincing you, change it – find the approach to riding that suits you.

As with so much in riding, there is no fixed right and wrong about riding on a contact – if it feels right in your heart, the horse is happy, it works, and you are in harmony with the horse, you are on the right track.

Things to do...

1. Have another go at exercise 1 in 'Things to do...' in Chapter 5, this time focusing on the QUALITY of the contact.

2. Go for a Western riding lesson, to show you what's possible without a constant contact. I know Western horses have a different carriage, but it is important to gather experiences and different 'feels'.

3. Try riding with no contact in walk, trot and canter, even if it's just on the lunge. The more you do this, the better your riding will become. The Spanish Riding School of Vienna lunges their trainee riders for months.

4. Pick the reins up slowly and gently, measure in your mind how much weight there is between your hand and the horse's mouth in pounds and ounces (grams and kilos if you REALLY have to!). See how much you can lighten the contact and still get the same results. See if you can have the same amount of weight in the reins for trot and canter as you do in walk.

5. Try to follow the horse's nod in walk, on the lightest rein you can, but with the reins looking like two sticks. Do this without looking. If you look you will never improve your feel, and feel is essential.

6. Establish in your mind exactly what your reasons are for having a contact; what the aim of it is that day; and how much contact you really need.

7. Read Chapter 5 on hands and wrists, Chapter 18, 'To be or not to be 'on the bit', Chapter 19 on taking lessons, and just about every other chapter.

Quick reference...

Have the contact as light as it can be, but as firm as it has to be; sometimes ride without contact; learn to follow the horse's mouth; know in your mind what you want to achieve with the contact, and why; use a passive feel; be adaptable with the amount of contact; imagine the horse's mouth is your mouth; think about regular rhythm; open the front door to go forwards.

Chapter 7

Is a bird, is it a plane, or is it an aid?

The aids are basically the language we use to communicate our ideas to the horse when we ride. The word 'aid' is an interesting choice; according to the dictionary it means to give **support**, **help** or **assistance**. So the aids aren't commands or orders, they are:

1. A way of giving **support** to our ideas of what we are asking the horse to do.

2. A way of **helping** the horse to understand what we want,

3. A way of **assisting** him physically to carry out our wishes.

Well, that sounds very nice and harmonious, but the truth is you can't force a 500kg, powerful, fast-moving animal to do much at all if it doesn't want to, and quite often, the more you try to force them with ever-stronger 'aids', the less inclined they are to do it.

So aids are a way of assisting in the communication between the rider and the horse.

That's it!

The senses

The main sense that the aids use is touch: that is physical communication between horse and rider. The additional senses that can be used are hearing (saying 'whoa', clucking the tongue, saying 'walk-on', etc) and visual (for example, reading body language). Horses also use the sense of smell to communicate with each other, but that is beyond our capacity, except that it is sometimes said that horses can smell our fear, which I suspect is true. It also sometimes appears that horses have a 'sixth sense', almost an ability to read our minds as in ESP (extra-sensory-perception), which has not been proved. Call me a soft touch, but I'm willing to believe it!

Decision-making

Giving the aids is about constant moment-to-moment decision-making. It is about reacting in each moment to how the horse is responding, and asking the right thing in the right way at the right moment. As long as you keep it logical and don't get personally involved, then it's relatively simple.

Just think something like, 'What movement do I want here? Oh yes, a so and so. He feels ready to do it. I'll ask now. He's not quite done it, so I'll ask again more firmly. Ah yes, he's started doing it. I'll stop asking ...very nice horse this.'

When should I give the aids?

Ask yourself: 'Do I have the horse's attention right now?' Give the horse some help to be attentive to you before expecting responses to light, subtle aids.

Only give an aid when you want something, and only then when you know exactly what you want. Giving an aid just to 'trot' without knowing exactly what trot you want is a bit like just asking someone to go to the shops for you and not telling them which shop, what they are supposed to buy, how much they should spend and how many items you want. So know exactly what you want, then ask.

It is important, too, that you become aware of not giving any aids unintentionally. This happens a lot with leg aids, where riders go 'leg, leg, leg' habitually and the horse ignores it. Repeating the aids for no reason like that is not really an aid, it's more of a niggle.

Repeat the aids only as necessary: no more and no less.

Imagine you're a horse...

You don't speak English, and understand practically none of it.

What if the aid doesn't work?

If the horse isn't responding, he may not be listening.

Don't give an aid, not get a reaction and give up: that is the best way to teach horses that you aren't committed and you're not worth listening to. Moreover it teaches them that not responding to the aids is a very worthwhile approach because you give up asking anyway. Some horses, especially riding school horses, are brilliant at this!

If an aid doesn't work within the space of one of the horse's footfalls, stop giving the aid for a moment then repeat the aid a little more firmly and so on until you get what you want.

Now here's the important bit: as soon as the horse responds to your request, stop giving the aid, or it just becomes a niggle.

What is not an aid?

1. Constant kicking.

2. Constant pulling on the reins.

3. Sawing the reins from side to side.

4. 'Whacking' with a stick.

5. Forceful use of spurs.

6. Shouting.

7. Forceful pushing with the seat and back.

8. Surprises (horses don't like them!).

Surprises

Never surprise a horse with an aid: think and prepare first, even just for a moment, before you ask. If you surprise the horse it will either become confused and/or you will get an incorrect response, or before the horse reacts there will be a pause, while it tries to figure out what it was you wanted.

What is the best time to give the aids?

Generally speaking, the best time to give the aids is when the horse is in the right state, mentally and physically to be able to carry out your request easily.

Think of ways you can set things up to win, both for you and the horse. A win-win situation is real riding.

If he's off his head with excitement, inattentive and distracted or his body is all over the place, you may find that the aids are not so effective, so firstly you need to do something to get him back 'on message', before expecting ideal responses.

The timing of the leg aids is particularly important, since leg aids at the wrong moment in the horse's stride are incapable of having any physical effect at all.

So often you see riders wondering why their leg aids seem to be having little or no effect, despite their legs dropping off and sweat pouring off their furrowed brow with the effort. Often people get told by their teacher that their 'legs aren't strong enough' – but hang on a minute, I thought it was the horse that was supposed to carry the rider, not the other way round!

The most effective moment to give a leg aid is when the horse's hind leg is just leaving the ground, at which point a light leg aid gives him a tickle in the ribs and makes him take a deeper or quicker step with his hind leg on the same side.

Do you need to give aids all the time?

No!

How do I know how strong the aid should be?

The ultimate aim is for the aids to be so subtle as to be invisible to onlookers, so why not start now by always using the smallest aid you can to get the job done?

Every aid should begin as lightly as you would ideally like, whether you think it will work or not. Then repeat the aid as many times as necessary, increasing the level of firmness each time until you get the response you want, **THEN STOP GIVING THE AID**. Next time you need to give an aid, start lightly all over again etc. If you follow this procedure each time you give an aid, you will find that the horse will get more responsive, happier with you and more respectful of you.

Naturally there are times of difficulty or potential danger when you have to use more emphatic (firmer) aids and do not have the luxury of starting the aids lightly and politely working up through them.

A summary of the aids

1. Doing nothing whatsoever

Doing absolutely nothing can be an aid that tells the horse quite a bit, e.g. 'carry on doing exactly what you are doing', or 'stand here quietly doing nothing until I ask you to do something else'. Many horses find it quite difficult to stand around doing nothing, so they need you to give them an aid to do it! Sitting on a horse doing nothing isn't something you see people doing very often, and it can be quite difficult for the rider too.

2. Thoughts and intention

Horses are great at sensing our thoughts and responding to them. The challenge for us is to make our thoughts clear enough that the horse knows exactly what we want. If the horse is ducking from left to right and doesn't know where to go, it is often because we're not that clear in our minds either. The same goes for stopping, changing gear, speed, carriage or whatever else you want. If you are crystal clear in your mind about exactly what you want, you're ninety per cent there and the horse will know it.

A thought is the first aid to give every time you want to ask something. It should precede any physical aid, therefore making the physical aid more of a supporting action than a forcing action. The physical aids merely 'back up' the thought about what you want.

> If you are crystal clear in your mind about what you want, you're 90% there, and the horse will know it.

3. Eyeballs and body

Horses communicate with each other using these aids. The herd leader looks where she wants to go, her body reinforces her gaze and all the others go that way with her.

When you ride using focus, looking where you want to go and using tiny indications of your body to express what speed, gear change or direction you want, you become a very effective rider. Your body, seat and eyeballs are the physical centre from which all the other aids take their cue.

4. Legs

Since the rider's legs are lying against the horse's sensitive sides and have a lot of connection with his body, even when they are quietly doing nothing, the legs support what the body is asking. The legs also create the impulsion (forward urge) by asking the hind legs to take more active steps. The seat and body

> Sometimes it's surprising how light the aids can be and still get great, quality responses from the horse.

Just for fun, see what you can achieve using totally invisible aids.

do not create impulsion, even though you frequently see riders pushing and thrusting their hips forward with gusto.

5. Reins

The reins are another way of supporting your thoughts, eyeballs, body and seat. For example, when turning right or left, here is the natural sequence of the aids to turn: you decide where you want to go, you look with your eyeballs, your body, seat and legs turn and your hands turn too. **That's it!**

Here is the unnatural sequence to turn: you pull the inside rein back towards you. **That's not it!**

Likewise with stopping, the reins are used in conjunction with other aids, not just pulled backwards on their own. (See also Chapters 5 and 6, on contact.)

Things to do...

1. In order to give a leg aid at the right moment we need to be able to feel which leg the horse is using at any given time in walk, trot and canter. When you are on a horse, his legs are your legs and they are your connection with the ground. See Chapter 16, 'The three paces' for easy ways to learn how to do this.

2. A fun way to see how the timing of the leg aids works is to get a friend on their hands and knees on the carpet. (This is getting more interesting already!) Rest your hands lightly on either side of the tickly part of their ribs, the same as your legs would be on a horse. Now get the friend to 'walk on' and use your hands on them just as each 'hind leg' is leaving the ground: if your timing and touch is right, your friend will involuntarily scuttle across the carpet. If your timing is out, your friend will move like a lazy old horse. At first you may need to look at the friend's 'hind legs' to see when they are being lifted, but see if you can do it by feeling it, that way it will be easy to transfer that feeling to when you are on a horse.

3. Start to notice when you are giving aids unknowingly. Breaking the habit of going 'leg, leg, leg' without meaning to can be quite frustrating at first, but well worthwhile if you want to become a seriously good rider.

4. See how light your aids can be and still get the right response. If you practise this consistently, one day people will watch you ride in wonder at the fact that the horse does things for you, but they can't see how you are asking it. Now that is a worthwhile goal.

Quick reference...

Aids are not orders, they assist the horse in understanding what we want; every aid should be prepared with a clear thought; don't surprise the horse with the aids; only give aids when necessary; start out lightly and get firmer if you need to; STOP giving the aid the moment the horse responds.

Chapter 8

Go, stop and changing gear

You can't do much with a horse if you can't get it to go or stop – that's obvious – but contained within the broad parameters of go and stop there are endless subtle nuances and benefits. The finer points of go and stop give you control over the speed and balance of the horse, as well as being a barometer for how well you are communicating, listening to each other and what kind of partnership you are enjoying. Go and stop is also about forwardness, transitions, and half-halts.

Some thoughts on 'go'

Seven simple ideas on 'go'

1. Think about your intention to move off a few seconds before you ask.

2. Be clear in your mind, not only about what gait you want – walk, trot or canter – but also about exactly what kind of walk, trot or canter, what speed, etc. you are intending to ask for. 'Trot-on' is just too vague for the horse.

3. Look where you want to go, before, during and after the transition.

4. Soften your waist and seat so that they allow the horse to move off, rather than pushing the horse off with the seat. Horses weigh about 500kg, so to think you can push the horse with your little buttocks is fantasy (as well as being uncomfortable for the horse's back).

5. Open the front door, i.e. let your hands allow the horse to go forwards. He can't do it very easily if the reins are blocking him.

6. Think of your upper thighs falling away from your hips and let your soft lower legs stimulate the horse's sides as lightly as possible to ask him to move off. Touch lightly with a schooling stick behind the leg if nothing happens after a couple of seconds of the leg aid. Remember: less is more.

7. Keep the lower leg gently on and let the horse take you through the transition.

The accelerator trick (a way to get more 'go')

I would bet a fair pile of cash that even the slowest plod would go like a rocket if he had a hungry eight-foot tiger up his backside.

So here's what to do. Instead of nagging him with 'more trot, more trot more trot, please trot faster', around the school, visualise a gallop, or at least a respectable canter, away from that hungry tiger, right from the very first stride. Picture energy and GO! GO! GO! from moment one.

People who can't get a lazy horse moving out are often mystified when the horse goes freely forward with another rider, who is apparently doing very little to achieve it. This is often because, although they may think they want the horse to go and are using their legs so much they feel like dying salmon after spawning, deep down they are apprehensive about the horse really going forwards. Horses are amazingly perceptive at this level of subconscious thinking. Many horses kindly oblige by not 'going for it' if the rider is apprehensive. Once the rider is more committed to going freely forwards, the horse will go more easily.

Sometimes it is just a matter of looking ahead so that you give the horse the attitude that you are both going somewhere. Conversely, looking down makes the horse think you want to go to the place where you already are, so he obliges you by not moving.

Some thoughts on 'stop'

Seven simple ideas on halt

1. Think about the halt a few strides before you want it.

2. Passively stop moving your elbows, rather than your hands (which will stop

On a scale of 1 to 10, ask yourself how much fun **the horse** is having. See if you can get it up to at least 8, right now.

anyway if you stop moving your elbows).

3. Cease 'flowing' so much with your seat, but without clenching your 'cheek' muscles.

4. Breathe out loudly as you ask for the halt.

5. Deepen your legs and keep them passively on the horse's sides. This is important but hard to understand somehow.

6. Think of riding the horse forward into the already halted bit, rather than bringing the bit backwards to halt the horse. When the horse goes into the already halted bit he'll stop in a far nicer way than if he is 'pulled' to a halt.

7. If you can feel the horse's footfalls through your seat, pick a particular front foot and think of stopping that one foot. If that foot halts smartly, so will the rest of the horse!

Don't analyse how this works, just try it and you'll find that it does.

The stopping trick

Would you like to really improve your halts? If there were a 100-foot drop, an electric fence or a herd of angry-looking rhinos at a certain spot in front of you, the horse would probably focus on stopping a lot more smartly. So put that idea into your own mind, and your aids and commitment to having the horse respond will be magnified.

As your mind visualises, your body sends messages to the horse saying **'We'd better stop. There. Now!'** Not, 'Sort of stop gradually over there somewhere when you feel like it', but **'Stop! Rhinos! There! Pointy horns! Now!'**

Even better, instead of thinking of stopping at a certain point, think of going backwards.

> If my horses are unresponsive or sloppy when I ask for stop, I will sometimes rein-back a few steps, or even back to the spot where I asked for halt, followed by a whole minute or two of rest on that spot as a reward.

The idea of letting the horse rest for a minute or two when he has halted is a brilliant way to teach horses to do better halts. After a few times you will find that the horse will be waiting to be allowed to halt for a rest, and the halts will become far more harmonious between you.

Some thoughts on 'Stop – Oh no, I've changed my mind. Carry on, please' (otherwise known as the 'half-halt')

If you think about stopping, momentarily begin the halting process and then continue to ride forwards, you will have carried out a half-halt. It is an ideal way to forewarn the horse of a forthcoming transition or new instruction, and it helps to rebalance the horse. If you don't feel any reaction whatsoever from the horse to your instruction to 'Stop – Oh no, I've changed my mind. Carry on, please', then try going back to doing more full stops and starts to sharpen him up.

▶ **Use the 'stopping trick' to rebalance or slow the horse down.** Instead of physically **trying** to get a rushing horse to go slower, and having only a modicum of success, visualise a transition down a whole gear or two. If you want to slow the canter, visualise a walk or even a halt, then just as you feel the horse about to fall out of canter, think, 'Oh, I've changed my mind. Stay in this nice slow canter, please.'

▶ **If the trot is too hurried and on your hands**, think about stopping. Just as the horse starts falling out of trot, think, 'Oh, that feels like a nice steady trot pace. I'll have that. Thanks very much. Carry on.' If the pace speeds up again, just visualise the same process. Pretty soon you should be able to control the tempo with much lighter physical aids, and much less hand, sweat and tears.

▶ **If the horse is really not listening to your ideas** you may need to engage the use of his own mind in the process of achieving a stop or slow-down. If the horse wants to keep moving his legs too fast, you could try putting him on a smallish circle or figure of eight, with a **passive** open rein, your legs quietly on him and your attitude one of waiting for him to slow. As he goes round and round, it probably won't take long before his mind realises that, although his legs are putting in lots of effort, he's not actually going anywhere! Instead of you trying to slow him, he may well decide that slowing would be good idea after all.

The metronome in your head

This is a very important concept, and not something many people give much thought to. It is also a very powerful tool for the rider.

The alternative way for the rider to control the tempo is by focusing on the

Notice if the horse tries to alter the speed. Resist the temptation to go along with the horse by sticking to the metronome in your head.

entirely physical means of legs, body and reins. You may think that there is no appreciable difference between these approaches, but horses work far better for a rider with a regular metronome in their head.

Tempo, **rhythm** and **speed** are essential for good performance. The tempo can be set by the horse, or by the rider, chiefly the rider's mind. Horses often try to set the tempo to suit themselves, and if the horse sets the tempo it is often inconsistent, sluggish or hurried, with the horse not having to balance or use himself properly. That is why it is important for the rider to have a metronome that doesn't change, ticking away in his or her head.

Try trotting with a metronome ticking in your mind. Fit into its tempo with your entire being as you rise or sit to the trot and see if the horse also fits into it. Make the speed comfortable for both of you. Do the same in canter.

Forwardness, impulsion and balance

People talk a lot about forwardness (or impulsion) – 'get him going forward', 'as long as he's going forward', etc. – but forwardness at the expense of balance, or at a tempo that is too much for the rider to sit comfortably to, is of little use.

▶ **Impulsion is not** a horse that naturally goes fast, or faster than the rider is requesting.

▶ **Forwardness has nothing to do with speed**. In the piaffe, for example, the horse trots slowly on the spot, but contained within the correct piaffe should be a desire and energy to go forwards that is like a coiled spring.

The ideal state of forwardness is when the horse responds smartly to the aid to move off, at precisely the tempo the rider asks for (not faster or slower), and giving the rider the feeling that the horse is 'under' the rider's seat, rather than running out from under the saddle.

It is easier for the horse to be forward and **not** keep his back under the rider than it is to stay in balance with the rider (you see this quite often, when the rider is sitting to the trot, struggling to absorb the horse's hard bouncy movement and giving the impression of being slightly towed along by the reins). It is far easier to ride a horse that stays under you than one that doesn't: paradoxically it can be quite difficult to get a horse to stay under you and go forwards. (If that lot made your head spin, don't worry about it. It's a feeling, and if you let it soak in you will start to get the feeling, honestly.)

The way to begin to achieve this feeling of the horse staying under you whilst going forwards is by getting the horse and yourself really good at go and stop. The more the horse gives you smooth, smart, upward and downward transitions on the lightest of aids, the more you will experience the feeling of the horse going truly forwards, staying in balance and at the same time not running out from under you.

Quiet transitions

Most of us 'do' too much and ask too loudly for transitions, particularly when going in or out of canter. See how quietly you can ask the horse to move up or down a gear. Try it just with your mind, breath and soft aids. Give the aids and wait a few seconds for the horse to try for you. When you feel the horse try, let him know he has done the right thing by ceasing to ask him.

One of the things that hinders good transitions is all the unconscious preparations that our bodies like to do. In effect, our bodies try to gate-crash the 'transition party' by getting all 'ready' and tense, especially when it's a 'canter transition party': 'Ooh, we're going to ask for canter ... getting a bit tight all over ... a little tighter in the back, legs, chest, arms and hands ... breathing a bit pinched ... here we go ... here we go now ... yeah! We're off into canter, kind of.'

Keep part of your mind quietly checking that your body is doing nothing unnecessary or uninvited before and through transitions. Try to pretend to your body and to the horse that you aren't going to do anything exciting or sudden like a canter transition, then quietly ask and then wait for him to respond.

> With your body, whisper to the horse to move up into trot or canter.

> Try to pretend to your body and to the horse that you aren't going to do anything exciting or sudden like a canter transition, then quietly ask and then wait for the horse to respond…

Remember: less is more

The more quietly you can ask for transitions, the smoother they will become. You don't just want a horse to go, stop or change gear any old how –that's like being in a car with a learner driver, pretty soon it gets boring having your neck wrenched back and forth as they dump the clutch, 'Ouch!' If you get a smooth transition, the new pace will also be smoother.

Think first, then ask

As stated before, horses don't like surprises, so instead of surprising them with the aids, and then wondering why they didn't respond very well, always think about exactly what you want first... every time! This may seem pretty obvious, but you'll be amazed at the difference 'thinking first' makes, and how often we forget to do it. The only real difficulty with 'thinking first' is remembering to do it, the rest is easy. 'Stop now.' There, that surprised you didn't it? You read it and thought 'what?' Far better if I'd forewarned you with 'I'm going to ask you to stop in a moment, OK stop now please.' MMmmmmm, that was better for both of us.

When I want to move off again, I don't just go 'TROT NOW.' Better to think 'I'm going to ask for trot in a moment, I'll want you to ooze into a steady working pace, with a rounded carriage and a soft contact, ready then?... "Trot-on." MMMmmmm!'

One of the main advantages of 'thinking first' is that it makes your aids more effective and lighter and the horse more responsive. How? Well, instead of the aids asking the horse to do a particular movement, your mind does the asking, and your aids merely back-up your request.

The more you do this, the more responsive the horse will be and the quicker he will respond.

Things to do...

1. Do lots of transitions!

2. Experiment with thinking about what you want first every time, until it becomes habitual.

3. Play around with the accelerator trick and the stopping trick.

4. Try riding with an awareness of the metronome in your head.

5. Practice thinking about stopping for a moment when you want the horse to slow down.

Quick reference...

Go and stop are essential and easy to improve; a horse that does go and stop very well will be better balanced and have better rhythm; preparation for transitions is essential; have a metronome in your head; forwardness or impulsion is not about speed.

Chapter 9

Effective steering

Steering a horse is not just about getting it to go where you want it to go. Contained within the details of correct steering are so many elements of more advanced work, lateral movements and the quality of carriage, and horse and rider communication. I have tried below to simplify some of the foibles of steering, which so many people seem to struggle with. Our human brains, coupled with the fact that when we are first taught to ride we are often taught to pull the inside rein to turn, sometimes find it difficult to let go of the active pulling approach to steering. Hopefully this chapter will begin to loosen the grip of some of the preconceptions about steering horses.

There are five classic rein positions, but it is not necessary or appropriate to detail all of them here. The first position is the 'direct' rein, an exaggerated version of which is the 'open' rein.

Open rein

Learning to guide horses effectively with an open rein is immeasurably useful: it can be used out hacking, during warming up and cooling down, for young horses and difficult or highly strung horses who aren't ready to accept a contact.

The open rein means that if you wish to turn right, you bring the right rein out away from the horse's neck and very slightly forwards. What happens is

Make sure that what you're asking the horse to do is made as easy as possible for him.

that the open rein creates a space into which the horse is invited to move. They normally find this invitation almost irresistible. There is no sense of pulling back on the horse's mouth.

The important things about an open rein are that the rein goes forwards and out (not out and backwards towards your leg) and that you look with your eyes and body in the direction you want to go. It is useful to let the other rein lie gently against the horse's neck, which supports the open rein by suggestion (horses can feel a fly on their skin, so they can definitely feel a rein against the neck) and it also starts to teach the horse about more subtle signals such as 'supporting rein', 'rein of opposition' and 'neck-reining'.

So remember, think and look where you want to go, turn your body slightly, bring the rein forward and out away from the horse's neck in an inviting fashion.

Using the 'open rein' in a much less exaggerated way is otherwise known as the 'direct' rein, so as you get a feel for the open rein, try refining it down to almost nothing, and see if the horse still responds to your request to turn.

Steering with both reins together

This is so much simpler than most people make it. To get the right feel, walk along on the ground (without a horse) with your elbows by your sides and your hands in the riding position. Now walk around to the right in one piece, i.e. without twisting at the neck or waist. What did your hands do? That's right, they just turned together with the rest of you – nothing different, nothing difficult, nothing more and nothing less. That's all you have to do on a horse – usually!

Learning to steer with both reins is technically tricky if you start to think about it too much, but to get great results in riding, you need to be able to turn the horse without using the inside rein more than the outside rein. Turning the horse's head more than you can bend his body breaks the natural arc which makes the horse round nicely and work correctly. Turning the horse's head more than his body also gives the horse an escape route, by which he can let his energy and impulsion fall out of one of his shoulders.

Imagine you're a horse...

You live in the moment and mostly choose to go in the direction of what is most comfortable.

It is important to note that the outside rein should not come to the inside so far that it crosses over the wither.

Faith and inside-reinitis

I have found that everyone can learn to turn without the inside rein within one lesson, as soon as they THINK they can do it and have faith that the horse will turn with both reins, not just by turning his head. Inside-reinitis is a very prevalent disease, to which many riders find themselves extremely attached.

Here is an exercise to help you achieve steering with both reins without even realising.

Try this exercise in walk in the school first:

Ride from letter F to B, then, keeping the horse's head and neck straight and doing as little as possible, see if you can turn left and ride across the school to letter E. Experiment with these turns, remembering that for the purpose of the exercise it is more important to keep the horse's head and neck straight and **think** of making the turn than to get a turn any old way. Even if it means that the horse doesn't go exactly where you want at first, gently keep his head and neck straight. You will soon get the feel of it.

As you get good at this exercise and start doing smaller school circles, you will find that the horse starts to come softly onto the bit.

Canal banks and eyeballs!

Here is some imagery to help make steering mystifyingly easier. Think of both hands and both legs forming two canal banks, one along the left side of the horse and one along the right, and think of the horse as being the water. Canal banks hold the water between them but do it totally passively – you never see canal banks moving about and trying to keep the water in, the water just stays there. You might say. 'Well, the water doesn't try to escape', but water, like a horse, is always ready to escape out through the path of least resistance: the banks just passively keep it in.

Now that the horse is there between the canal banks of your passive hands and legs, you simply use your eyeballs to let him know in which direction you want his energy and his body to go, like the flow of the water.

> Create a partnership of cooperation between you and the horse.

Many people find it hard to remember to look where they're going when they ride. It might help if you always think: **'Look to the horizon, both on a horse and in life!'**

Weight and legs

Concentrate on your upper body staying upright through turns and circles, not tipping in or out.

Many people get confused by thinking about putting weight here and there and 'using' the inside leg to turn the horse. Whilst there is some truth in these ideas, they become grossly exaggerated and misunderstood.

The amount of weight used to turn is so tiny that it is best to forget about it altogether and allow your body to 'learn' unconsciously what is most effective. Intentionally putting weight one way or the other to turn makes it more difficult for the horse to maintain his centre of balance through the turn. To help the horse the most, try to sit as centrally as you can through your turns.

Likewise 'using' the inside leg to turn: think only of subtly stepping down a shallow stair with the inside foot (an invisible aid) and you will help the horse far more than trying to squeeze him around the corner in a way that makes no sense whatsoever to him or you, if you think about it.

The simple answer is: if you want to turn the horse, just turn yourself!

Things to do...

1. Practise riding using an open rein when things are going well, so that you can call upon the use of the open rein with ease in any situation. Remember, it is often better to do that than grab the reins and make the horse feel more panicky.

2. Try turning without a horse, holding your hands in the 'rein position'. Really learn how this feels.

3. See if you can refine the open rein so that it is almost non-existent, and still get the same results with the horse.

4. Try turning the horse by keeping the outside rein straight (like a stick) and letting the inside rein go slightly slack. This will give you more new 'feels'.

5. Start by riding a 20m circle (say, to the left) with the horse's head bent softly to the inside (the left) using an open rein. As you cross the centre line flow into a 20m circle going the other way (around to the right) but maintain the horse's head bend still softly to the left. Finish off by going back to the original circle to the left. Repeat the whole exercise on the other rein.

This exercise is great for gently suppling the horse, but it is also brilliant for getting the rider to shift out of the preconceived belief that the horse's head has to be pulled to the inside.

Quick reference...

Less is more; practise using an open rein; turn with both reins the same; canal banks and eyeballs! Turn your whole self as one piece and trust the horse will turn; think a lot less about the physical mechanics of turning and just do it.

Part 3

Mindwork

Riding is not only a physical activity, but a mental and emotional one too. This fact is often overlooked. Whether you are learning something new, improving your performance as a rider, building confidence, or training a horse, making the best use of your mind and the horse's mind is the fast-lane to getting results with far less sweat and tears.

Learning to use mindpower with horses can carry over into every area of our lives. Relating better to horses can help us to relate better to other people, whether they are loved ones, business clients, employees and employers, complete strangers or even ourselves!

The only aid that should be active all the time whilst riding is not the leg, hand or seat, but the mind: it is the most powerful, effective and often the most neglected aid at the disposal of the rider. Without using the mind, riding is nothing more than an ungraceful exercise in pushing and pulling a poor four-legged beast about.

Chapter 10

Positive attitude

You may think that positive thinking and NLP are just trendy 'buzz-words', or that you've heard about that kind of stuff and it's obvious: but it is a fact that riders with a confident and positive attitude get far better results with horses than riders with more 'riding ability' and a negative outlook. Horses will naturally follow a positive leader (but not a bully), whether that leader is human or equine. Our own bodies also perform better when we have a positive attitude.

How do we get a more positive attitude, without deluding ourselves into thinking we're totally, unrealistically, dangerously marvellous?

If you want a more positive attitude you can build it, despite your mind telling you that it's all lies and you can't change the way you are.

Seven steps to building a positive attitude

Step 1 – Focus on every small success

Expect less from the horse and yourself, and be pleased with the slightest success. Even half a circle or a halt done perfectly well is an achievement; for anyone to do these things perfectly with a horse is a challenge. Notice the little

If you don't have all the answers you need, ask the right questions! Contained within the question lies the answer ...

things that go well and remember them. Learn to see the tiny elements of progress and be pleased. Tiny elements of progress are how most training happens with horses and riders. Remember what the good moments felt like at the time, so that you can reproduce them.

Step 2 – Leave the negative things behind – move onwards and upwards

Don't beat yourself up over things that go badly. If you never made any mistakes, you'd never learn. We all learn from mistakes (actually, learning from other people's mistakes is far less painful!), but it's best not to get attached to mistakes and keep playing them over and over like a favourite video tape. As you leave the stables or the manège, drop all the things that went badly into an imaginary rubbish bin, and leave them there, never to be seen again.

Step 3 – Just because it happened before, it doesn't mean it'll happen every time

Remember that, like life itself, every moment of riding is unique: just because your horse shied at an imaginary Tyrannosaurus Rex last time doesn't mean it will happen every time. Picture things going well this time. Develop 'selective amnesia', where you can't remember the T-Rex episode at all, even if the horse tries to remind you of it. Learn to bounce back, but not by repeatedly risking your neck or allowing frustration or failure to overwhelm you. Just move the goal-posts and have another go.

Step 4 – What your thinker thinks, your prover proves

Start to really notice the things you think and say. I have often met people who say things like, 'Oh, I hope this horse won't buck with me, because horses **always** buck with me.' The horse, which is not usually a bucker, bucks like stink with them for the whole ride! Or, 'Oh, this horse won't bolt with me, will it?' And there it goes off over the horizon, leaving its brains and its friends a mile

Thinker = conscious mind
Prover = subconscious mind

Instead of panicking, ask yourself: 'What can I **do** now?'

behind, when normally it's the stable-yard sloth!

None of us likes to appear to be an idiot or be proved wrong (even to ourselves), so having said that a certain thing will happen, our subconscious tries to make it happen. That way, we **prove** what we said was right! It seems bizarre, but it's true. Noticing all the limiting or self-defeating things you think and say is a **BIG** step towards making real progress.

Step 5 – Use positive statements to make good things happen

The next step is obvious: get your 'thinker' to think the right things, and your 'prover' will make the right things happen! Easy, hey?

(Of course, you may think this is all twaddle, and you are entitled to your opinion. What's more, if you think that, I guarantee that your 'prover' will be busy proving you're right, and that it is twaddle.)

Think things like: 'I can hold this horse', 'I can get over that jump', 'I'm relaxed and comfortable riding out', 'It's easy to get good transitions to canter', 'It's easy to get horses on the bit', 'I can easily learn this', 'I trust my seat, I'm really good at staying in the saddle', 'I really trust this horse', 'Flying changes are easy when I let them happen', 'When I'm soft, the horse goes soft', etc.

Step 6 – Have only positive teachers and people around you

Don't listen to people who put you down. Some teachers should be shot at dawn for constantly giving only criticism and negative feedback. They are actually being paid to make your riding **WORSE**! (Teaching and getting the most from lessons is a whole subject on its own which we'll look at in Chapter 19, on taking lessons).

Friends and people around you may make jokes that can unintentionally have a negative effect on your attitude. An example might be, 'Oh yes, Agnes, you always get the bucker/ rearer/ bolter/ ****er/ kicker don't you?' Such comments feed a negative programme into your subconscious, which you don't need. Politely ask them not to say it, ignore their jesting, or avoid them altogether.

Don't measure your progress by what others are doing, or even by competition judges; the true measure of progress is how many joyful, fun and beautiful moments you and the horse can create together.

Step 7 – Start believing in yourself

Telling yourself you can do it, other people telling you that you can do it, visualising yourself doing it and seeing yourself succeed in small ways all go towards building an ability to believe in yourself. Set up these patterns, even for say three weeks or a month to give it a try: see how it works, stick at it and you can do it. See this period as an exciting challenge, filled with fun and interesting discoveries about yourself.

Positive thinking and reality: a word of warning

Horses are big, strong and unpredictable: that's a fact.

Positive mindpower really works: that's a fact too.

So take the middle road – don't do dangerous things just because you think you can! Use common sense at all times around horses. Ask yourself if you and the horse are ready to cope. For example, don't try mounting an unbroken horse for the first time when there's a gale blowing, someone's erecting a tent twenty-five yards away, the neighbouring farmer is feeding his pigs, or you're upset because your lover just ran off with a Masai warrior. Developing your 'intuition' will help with knowing how much to take on.

Things to do...

1. Start reprogramming old thought patterns. Notice when you say or think words like 'can't', and when you think or say things like 'I'm useless at that', 'I'll never be able to do that', 'That's my worst thing', 'This is really difficult', 'It'll take me ages to be able to do that', 'I always fall off when I …' etc.

   The first step is to notice when you do it, and then stop yourself, preferably before the words come out. If the words do come out, say another sentence straight afterwards that puts you 'back in credit'. For example, cancel out 'Oh, I always fall off when I'm jumping,' by saying 'I'm good at staying on when jumping.'

   Start a 'negative comment penalty box', so that every time you say something negative about your riding, you put a £1 fine in the box. At the end of every month spend it on a treat or give it to a horse charity.

2. The more positive experiences you build up, the more positive you will

become: it's that simple. For example, if you want to do well in competitions, or to beat your competition nerves, don't go straight for the big shows, go to a tedious number of small shows, where you can do well time after time, gradually increasing the scale of challenges.

3. Develop a more generous attitude to yourself and the horses you ride, not by giving them carrots or yourself more chocolate, but by enjoying small successes, and not pushing hard for results and goals all the time. Remember that riding is for pleasure, hopefully for the horse and the human. Horses don't share our ambitions, they just get roped into them.

4. Accept that riding is AT LEAST FIFTY PER CENT a mental game, and as soon as you realise it you can move your game up to new heights.

Quick reference...

Using the mind can be a powerful aid; horses respond to a positive leader; you can reprogramme negative thought patterns; build a credit account of positive experiences.

Chapter 11

Developing infinite patience

Horses are very emotional creatures – they get very carried away with excitement or fear. Riders too can be very emotional creatures, getting carried away with wanting to win, staying on board, getting a result, controlling the horse, jumping higher, stopping a run-away.

Can you imagine how much more effective and powerful you would become with horses if you remained 'emotionally uninvolved'? If everything you did was well timed, decisive and deliberate, like a 'Jedi master'?

Losing your patience is an example of getting 'emotionally involved' in the situation. Learning to have infinite patience is one of the essential foundation stones of mastery.

Patience

If there is one thing you need by the truckload to be around horses, it's patience. You need it almost every time you go near a horse. You need to be

Imagine you're a horse...

You're not interested in money, saving for a rainy day, the future, pensions, winning rosettes, fame or material things.

Imagine you're a horse...

You are very sensitive, mentally and emotionally, although this is often misunderstood.

patient with horses, and you need to be patient with yourself. Then just when you think you're incredibly patient, you need to be even more patient. The fact is, and this is not used here just as a figure of speech, **you need to have infinite patience to be good with horses.**

Riding and patience

▶ The nice thing about developing more patience is that you become kinder to yourself as well as the horse.

▶ Being unjust or impatient with a horse can leave you feeling like a real 'so-and-so'. Being patient leaves you feeling good about yourself, horses and life, and helps you to progress quicker

▶ The moment we lose our patience with a horse, we show him we're not as solid as he thought we were, and we probably aren't worthy enough to be his leader after all.

▶ As soon as our patience goes, we stop making good decisions, and our actions become clouded by our annoyance.

▶ Being impatient involuntarily tightens your body, making it more difficult to ride well. That's another good reason to develop infinite patience.

▶ Along with patience, or a lack of it, is what is termed 'end-gaining'; this is where all your attention and desire is set on achieving the end result or the outcome you want, without giving enough attention to the process(es) involved along the way. With riding, this is a very easy trap, and one that we all fall into now and again. Performance in competition can be truly enhanced when the rider focuses on 'the job in hand', rather than focusing on the desperate desire to win.

Patience is not a limited aspect of our characters: by using mindpower it can be consciously developed and increased. Here is how...

Ten steps towards developing infinite patience

1 – Only bite off what you can chew

Only ask things of the horse or yourself that you can both cope with, and that won't take longer to work through than you have time for.

How do you know whether something will be too much for you before you try it? Well, although you need to challenge yourself in order to progress, it is usually best to ask for a little, be pleased, and then ask a little more. Let your inner common sense help you to decide what is safe, sensible and reasonable to ask **that** horse, on **that** day, in **that** situation. If in doubt, ask for less.

> PATIENCE, PATIENCE, PATIENCE will always be rewarded with horses. (If you're patient enough to wait for it.)

2 – Act as if you have all the time in the world

If something is taking a long time, tell yourself you have all day and all night and all the next day; you just don't mind. If you really don't have all day, leave it for a time when you have. Horses seem to have a feel for when you have all day, and they usually oblige in a couple of minutes. Horses also seem to have a feel for when you are pressed for time, and they can become incredibly unhelpful. If you can't appear to have all day, forget it!

3 – Be kind and persistent

Make corrections in a kind and quiet way, but always be more persistent than the horse.

4 – Smile a lot

Smiling will give you a nonchalant attitude. Whistling or humming also helps.

5 – Develop your confidence

Patience develops by having confidence. If you are confident that you will achieve your goal there is no reason to lose your patience, since you know you will succeed eventually ... even if it takes you 'til next Christmas!

Confidence comes from being competent, recognising every small success, knowing your own limitations (not the ones other people try to set for you), developing physical skills, and only biting off what you feel you can chew.

6 – Accept that 'horses will be horses'

Many people lose their patience with horses because they think the horse is 'playing them up', or 'messing them about', whereas the horse is just behaving within its nature. Try to find the reason for the horse's behaviour: mostly it is just the horse acting like a horse. Once you realise that fact, it can save you going red in the face, pulling your hair out and using up too many of your valuable heartbeats too quickly.

7 – Stop your impatience BEFORE it runs away with you

As soon as you feel your patience putting its skis on and stepping onto that familiar slippery slope, stop what you're doing and ask yourself, 'What will I achieve here by losing my patience?' Answer: **ABSOLUTELY NOTHING**.

Then ask yourself, 'Will the horse respect me more for losing control of myself?' Answer: **NO**.

Stop what you are doing, take a few moments to compose yourself, get off the slippery slope of impatience, take your skis off, and congratulate yourself for being such a well-controlled individual, worthy of the title, 'horseman'.

8 – Accept that riding takes a lifetime to master

Remember that it takes many, MANY hours for anyone, even experts, to train a horse to be a good all rounder.

Be patient with yourself about the progress of your riding. Accept that learning to ride well and becoming good with horses takes years. It takes everyone masses of time to learn the physical skills, mental agility, emotional balance, background knowledge, lightning responses, etc. to be really good. However much time you spend riding and being with horses, there will still be mountains of things left to learn. Remind yourself that it takes many years for experts like the Spanish Riding School of Vienna to train riders.

> You can be impatient as a novice or impatient as an advanced rider – your level and experience won't alter how patient you are.

9 – Be the master of your mind, not the victim of the situation

Being patient is just a state of mind. Most of the time we cannot change the situation, but if we are willing to, we can change our state of mind about how

'Bananas': a story about patience

I never thought I was very patient until I ended up with a horse we called Bananas. I had only glanced at Bananas over the stable door, and not seen her handled at all before her arrival at my yard. She was a stunning, young, 'unbroken' Spanish horse, and when she arrived it became evident why she had been so reasonably priced. We couldn't do a thing with her, and I mean a thing! Thus she was named Bananas.

At this time I had started a fair few youngsters with the 'advance and retreat' method in the round-pen, so off Bananas and I went to the round-pen. This horse was so disturbed she would have run until she died, rather than hook up with me. I made a few more attempts, but every day was the same. In the following months, I proceeded to try every method and idea I could think of to get this horse to be less like her namesake.

It became a supreme test of patience and emotional control. There was never a question of me ever 'losing it', as this horse was so emotionally on the edge. It seemed it would be impossible for her to be sold, except for slaughter, so I carried on.

During the whole time that things were completely hopeless, and she was nowhere near ready to even sit on, I kept visualising myself riding this beautiful Spanish horse around the pen in a relaxed canter, with her neck arched, and with me sitting easy with one hand on the reins. It seemed like a total fantasy at the time.

After a year of working with this horse almost every single day she was finally allowing us to ride her in walk, trot and canter; she wasn't really happy about it, but it was still a triumph of patience.

One day at the end of this year my patience was truly rewarded in an unexpected way. After riding Bananas out, I sat on the garden seat with her in a halter in front of me. I spent the whole afternoon idly chatting with a friend, and holding Bananas' muzzle in my hands, giving it no thought whatsoever. The next day my wife rode her out, and said 'Bananas is a different horse. What have you done to her? She's happy to be ridden!' She was a different horse and was happy to be ridden from that day onwards, and still is. I don't know if I could have started this horse any quicker, though I dare say there are people who could. I have brought other youngsters to the same point in a few days; Bananas had taken a year. It was a great lesson in patience for me, and although she turned out to be a wonderful riding horse, I have absolutely no desire to do it ever again.

we view the situation. That makes the whole thing seem totally different. And if it seems totally different, then we **have** changed it! This really works with horses.

10 – Don't let things get too scary

People sometimes appear to lose their patience with horses because they feel threatened or scared. If you feel like this, take on less of a challenge. Go back to where you feel confident you can cope. For example, if you notice yourself getting more impatient when jumping, go back to doing more flatwork, maybe put in the odd small jump or two, then leave it at that. Gradually accustom yourself to the things that make you feel edgy: Rome wasn't built in a day, and patience is no different. Be kind to yourself and the horse, and it will all come right in time.

Some thoughts about anger

Anger is when fear or impatience has escaped, and is running loose in the top paddock!

People get angry around horses a lot, and although it's easy to say and not so easy to do, there is just no point in getting angry around horses.

My first lesson in this was when breaking in a young stallion. I had got angry at horses in the past with no problem, but with a stallion things can be quite different. I could be very firm with him provided it was done without anger and injustice, but if I did anything in anger, a different look would enter his eye. Unless I immediately put aside the anger, I was in some seriously deep muck.

Horses sense the unnecessary injustice of being on the receiving end of a human's anger.

We need to learn to control our anger to have a ghost of a chance of forming a harmonious partnership with 500kg of flighty beast.

Anyway, what right do we have to take our anger and frustration out on these basically timid creatures, and what does it say about us as people if we do?

If you start feeling angry, and can't let it go, leave whatever you're doing with the horse for another day.

I found this wonderful quote in an old American training manual:

'If you cannot or will not control your temper at all times, then let someone else school your horses, before you ruin them.'

Things to do...

1. Practise being patient whilst sitting in traffic or standing in a queue. See if you can find it amusing that you can be held up there, and not get wound up. You may even find that you start to giggle when you manage to do this.

2. Give yourself more time to spend with horses than you normally allow. Instead of rushing up to the stables, riding the horse for an hour and then rushing off again, spend some time 'hanging out' with the horse, maybe give him a massage, ride for less time, asking less than usual, and then 'hang out' again for ten minutes on the ground. You get better results this way than just getting on and working the horse. He'll notice that you're less impatient about the time or getting results; he'll enjoy being with you more, so he'll help you to get better results.

3. Take up yoga, meditation or the Alexander Technique, as ways of developing more mindpower. These are all tried and tested methods that really work if you stick at them, and they will definitely improve your riding, self-control, anger and patience management and many more areas. They may also make you even more wonderful to live with!

4. Ride within your limitations, so that you always feel more mentally in control of the situation. Your riding will still improve, and so will your patience, nerve, fear levels, ability to think things through, etc.

5. Learn from others: watch people with their horses, especially at shows or competitions, and see how their lack of patience actually makes it more difficult for them to cope with the horse or the situation. Remind yourself not to do that.

6. Have a think about ways that you end-gain when you ride: and even how you might start to end-gain before even getting on the horse or arriving at the stables!

Quick reference...

It is best to stay emotionally uninvolved around horses; you need infinite patience to achieve the best results; patience gives you more personal power and makes horses respect you more; you can build patience step by step; keep smiling, keep trying, keep your cool.

Chapter 12

Using role models

J ust imagine you are planning to ride a horse for the very first time, but you have never seen anyone else ride a horse before in your life. You really wouldn't know where to start, and nor would any of us! By copying other people we learn what is possible in life, learn how to learn, how to take short-cuts and how to improve faster. This is called 'modelling'.

Think how much you could learn and how quickly you could improve your riding by a really detailed and skilful use of modelling, not just by copying the physical methods of superior riders, but also by using mindpower to develop a similar mental attitude and 'feel'.

It follows that if you reproduce the same physical, mental and emotional attitudes as a highly successful rider or role model, you would produce similar results. Wow!

Our state of mind and body posture are intrinsically linked, so if you feel like a winner, you'll move like a winner, and if you move like a winner, you'll feel like a winner.

Everyone is different

Learning to see the differences

Why is it that rider A gets fantastic results and enjoys an almost magical rapport with horses, whereas rider B gets only mediocrity? If you could find out and analyse exactly what makes rider A more successful, you could copy his habits and theoretically enjoy similar results. I'll admit that sometimes it is hard to see what really brilliant riders are doing, because their aids are so subtle. Of course, it is not enough just to look at the rider you are modelling, you need to take action by practising ways to teach your body to recreate the images your mind is receiving.

Theoretically, if someone can perform in a certain way, then it is possible for anyone else to model that person and achieve similar results. If you had spent twelve years of daily training at the Spanish Riding School of Vienna, learning exactly the way the other trainees learn, chances are you'd look pretty good on a dancing white Lipizzaner stallion by now. The fact that the trainees learn by modelling their masters means that they benefit from 400 years of accumulated knowledge, experience and learning in a fraction of the time.

> Today, improve your performance by even 1% or 2% in five areas of your riding, and see how good you become.

Pick a hero

Think of a rider whom you really admire: please aim high by picking someone seriously brilliant (we're talking global, not local).

If I'm doing flatwork, for example, I might picture Carl Hester, Arthur Kottas or the late, great Nuno Oliviera. Look at every detail of how a superb rider sits and the position they adopt, use mindpower to get inside their body with your imagination, and see how it feels to ride like that person. Don't assume that just because they are the top riders, they always sit with perfection. You might learn quite a bit from seeing where they aren't entirely correct. It can be quite encouraging to realise that even the best aren't perfect.

Step out of yourself

One of the great things about modelling, or even just simply copying a great rider, is that it takes you out of yourself. That means you become mentally detached from yourself. You have put a space between what you are doing and your usual personal thoughts and limitations. Instead of thinking about my leg being far back enough, or my seat being too stiff, when you are modelling someone else, it becomes just 'a leg' and just 'a seat'. It is far easier to move 'a leg' back than it is to move my leg back, because I know that my leg doesn't

Imagine you're a horse...

You have times when you feel like playing, times when you feel like dozing, times when you feel emotional, times when you feel peaceful.

like going back! It is far easier to copy the upright posture of Carl Hester than it is for me to sit up straight, because I don't usually sit up straight, whereas Carl Hester always does, etc.

'Sofa riding'

Start to pinpoint what you think it is about your chosen hero that makes them special. As you look at your role model, really let your mind soak in the image, so that you start to feel as though you are actually inside their body.

If you aren't watching your role model in person, it doesn't matter. Just put on the TV or a video, sit on the edge of the sofa and copy their gestures and movements. Really move and act as if you were riding. (At least if you fall off the sofa it's a soft landing!). Have fun with this: the more you do it the more deeply the whole experience will be recorded in your memory and, therefore, the more successfully you will be able to recall it next time you are on a horse.

'Sofa riding' is often commonly carried out unconsciously (have you noticed how everybody breathes in and leans forward for the jumps while watching show jumping on the TV?), but we're going to use it consciously as a mindpower-ful tool to improve your ability to perform the task of riding.

Try asking yourself detailed questions about your role model's riding, such as:

▶ **How do they sit?**
  Do they have a toned upper body; do they sit slightly back, slightly forward?

▶ **Do they look like they are dominating the horse, or part of a six-legged being?**
  Is their back soft or braced?

▶ **Are their hands still, low, high, wide, firm, light, moving around, tense, soft?**
  Are their shoulders held up or relaxed down; is their chest braced, soft, still or moving?

▶ **Is their head still, balanced, held up or flopping about?**
  Does their seat hover over the saddle, drive the horse or move passively with the horse?

▶ **Is their face concentrated, smiling, relaxed, tense, gazing into the distance or looking worried?**
  Are their heels up, level or down?

▶ **Are their legs hanging loosely or firmly held; are the legs well back,**

under the hips or in front of the hips; do the legs look soft, firm, active or quiet?

...and so on.

We can feed an image of all of these things and more into our minds quickly and easily, and then begin to piece together how to emulate, reproduce and copy the rider we have looked at.

> Experiment with what effects you have on the horse by copying different role models. The horse is always your most essential source of feedback.

How does it feel?

So you know what your role model does with their body and what they look like, but what really makes a difference is how they think and feel. If you can get into the mental and emotional, as well as the physical state, of a highly successful rider you are on the path towards experiencing the same things as they do.

> Remember that mental state and body performance are intrinsically linked.

It is not always easy to access information about how top riders think and feel, but you can't imagine that they waste too much energy thinking how naff they are or how many things they can't do, or what if they fall off or lose a stirrup!

Focus on 'feeling the part'

Start to really focus on 'feeling the part'. If, say, your role model has said that say they feel 'inwardly calm and yet thinking clearly' when they perform at their peak, for example, try copying that mental attitude as precisely as you have tried copying their physical attitudes.

You may be thinking, 'Yikes, how do I do that?' It's easy ... all you need to do is recall a time when you felt 'inwardly calm and yet thinking clearly' yourself – and it may well have been when you were doing something other than

Reading interviews with successful riders is a great way to glean information about how they think, feel and prepare themselves for competitions.

riding, but that doesn't matter. Now adopt the same mental feeling or attitude while you ride. The more you practise this the easier it will get.

Playing around with this idea of really 'feeling the part' has an additional advantage: whilst you are thinking about being 'inwardly calm and yet thinking clearly', your old dis-empowering mental attitudes will start to break down. There will be no time or space left in your head for worries about things going badly wrong, not being good enough or not learning fast enough.

Things to do...

1. Keep in mind that riding is for fun and pleasure, no matter how many people seem to ride better than you!

2. Remember to have high standards when picking someone to model.

3. Develop the ability, through detailed analysis, to be able to put yourself into the body patterns and the mind states of successful riders.

4. Practise 'sofa riding'.

5. Play this game with some friends. Cut out some pictures of top riders and take them to the manege with you – one from each discipline, say showjumping, dressage, racing, western, classical riding, etc. Take it in turns to mime the photos on horseback, while the others try to guess which person you are copying. I guarantee you'll have a real laugh, but more than that, you will step out of yourself and discover new possibilities in the way you ride.

Quick reference...

Role modelling is a powerful way of improving your performance by copying someone else's physical, mental and emotional states; if someone else can do it, theoretically so can you; look at every detail; model the best of the best, project yourself into their body and mind; feel it, live it, have fun with it.

Chapter 13

Visualisation and imagination

As we saw earlier, whatever you focus your attention upon usually happens. Where your intentions are placed, your subconscious will obediently direct energy to that scenario, doing everything it can to make it actually come about in reality. **This is why it is so important and yet so powerful to visualise what you wish to happen, rather than imagining what you don't wish to happen.**

If you ride along thinking things will go wrong, or the horse might play up, or you might fall off, then your imagination is running amok and having a wild party. Instead of your imagination employing itself to create scary or negative scenarios, employ it yourself to imagine things going really well ... or even better than you have previously dared to imagine!

It's YOUR imagination, not its own or someone else's.

Be sure of one thing: if you don't give your imagination something to think about, it will start thinking of its own ideas – and it just loves to be scared. That's why we pay to watch scary movies at the cinema, crazy though it may seem.

Getting your imagination to work **for** you, rather than against takes a little practice. Like using a muscle that you perhaps haven't used for a while, it may seem odd, impossible, hard work or unrealistic at first, but as sure as horses are hairy, if you don't imagine things the way you want them, your imagination

Ask yourself: 'In
what way am I
limiting my riding or
this horse right
now?' Let the
answer come to
you.

will probably come up with something you definitely don't want. Remember that the movies 'Friday the 13th' and 'The Exorcist' were the products of someone's imagination!

Imagine yourself riding like a natural or like a winner, imagine easily doing that cross-country course, having that incredible collected canter, doing those flying changes, galloping off into the sunset, having a wonderful seat, gliding through that dressage test with top marks, being effective on every horse you ride.

You have nothing to lose and everything to gain by becoming the master, rather than the victim, of your own powerful imagination.

Things to do...

1. **THINK** about adjustments to your riding position, visualise yourself altering and riding more effectively and with poise.

2. Sit or lie somewhere comfortable and relaxed, with eyes closed, and visualise riding in a certain difficult situation, a particular movement or something you are having problems with. Feel every sensation, and imagine exactly how it would feel to do whatever it is really well. With practice, your brain will programme your body to be able to better carry out the task you are visualising. Get into the habit of imagining things going really well. I swear that if you do this, often things turn out even better than you'd imagined them.

3. Try consciously thinking about each movement or transition a good few strides ahead, clearly visualising what you are going to ask for. See what a positive effect it has on the communication level between you and the horse, and how much you can minimise your aids. See if it can become so subtle that observers can't see your aids. **NEVER** surprise a horse with your aids.

4. Have a go at using the visualisation 'tricks' as described in Chapter 8, 'Go, stop and changing gear', e.g. the steering trick, the stopping trick, etc.

5. Next time you ride, instead of **TRYING** to get more in harmony with the horse, allow yourself to be more in harmony. Keep a mental awareness of

staying emotionally balanced and unattached to what you and the horse are doing: anytime you feel one of those emotional pitfalls coming up (anger, worry, fear, impatience, end-gaining or frustration), say to yourself, 'LET'S DO SOMETHING DIFFERENT.' You may think that doing away with the emotional involvement will take away all the pleasure, but actually it will raise it to a level you never knew existed.

Quick reference...

Imagine things going well; do less and think more; think ahead of every new movement; tell yourself it's fun; tell yourself I **CAN** do this; visualise exactly what you want; make a commitment to yourself to over-ride any disempowering thoughts or images that your mind comes up with; ride within the capabilities of yourself and the horse; don't take unnecessary risks.

Chapter 14

Confidence and nerves

Riding can be such a fantastic, up-lifting experience, and horses such wonderful, noble creatures – the combination is pure food for the soul. One ride and you're hooked. But here's the catch: what if you love horses and riding so much that you can't give them up, but you lack the confidence or the nerve to experience the full enjoyment?

For so many people the joys of riding are tainted by feeling nervous, and for so many riders a lack of confidence holds them back from really fulfilling their potential.

Everyone gets nervous or scared around horses at some time or other – and if they say they don't they are either lying, crazy or both.

Now here's the good news: by replacing nervous or self-doubting thoughts with thoughts of confidence and self-belief, you become free to ride towards your dreams. It's as simple as that!

The confidence we want to build around horses needs to be on solid foundations. That means taking as long as it takes to progress, nurturing your confidence with care, avoiding bad experiences that set you back, and acquiring as much competence, knowledge and skill around horses as possible.

> **Time + Patience + Care + Competence + Good experiences + Encouragement = Confident rider**
>
> **Over-horsed + Bad experiences + Derision + Lack of Skill + Unrealistic goals = Nervous wreck!**

Ask yourself: 'If I were to allow myself to become a better rider right now, what would I do differently?' Now do it ... go on!

Some important definitions

▶ **Confidence**: having a belief in your own abilities; being self-assured. Belief in yourself is flexible, which means it can be built up.

▶ **Fear**: the feeling of distress or apprehension caused by the thought of possibly being hurt, whether it is likely to happen or not. The fear of something is very often worse than actually experiencing the thing we are afraid of.

▶ **Courage**: the ability to act despite your fear, so even if you feel nervous or fearful, you are still able to take action. Courage is therefore a totally individual quality. It may be courageous for one person just to walk into a horse's stable, and for another it may be to ride in the Grand National.

So, just because you feel fear doesn't mean you are not being courageous.

Ten tips for building confidence and conquering nerves

1 – Accept that it is OK to be nervous

Being nervous is a perfectly understandable and natural survival mechanism, therefore there is no need to feel embarrassed or annoyed with yourself. Accepting how much nerve you have is a good starting point on which to build confidence step by step. It's great having fun with horses, but it's no fun getting hurt: being cautious means you are not just 'being silly', you are being sensible.

If your mind is telling you what you are doing is not safe, maybe it is right! Unless you have developed a good seat and are riding a sensible horse in a situation you can manage, then being nervous seems quite reasonable.

There is never any real need for heroics around horses. It is far better to get

Imagine you're a horse...

You have the capacity to play and enjoy yourself.

off the horse and walk away than to get carted off by paramedics, having tried to prove something to yourself or other people.

Know your own mind, ignore peer pressure and don't compare your progress or ability with other people. Everybody is different: only measure your nerve and progress with yourself.

2 – Avoid being over-horsed and avoid situations you may not be ready to handle

Remember: horses are always 'for real'.

Sometimes it is good to be stretched by a healthy challenge in order to learn more, but that is quite different to being over-horsed. Far better not to challenge yourself (or your horse) too much than to lose the confidence that you have built up.

Even with little experience around horses you can start to trust your inner voice to tell you what you feel ready to handle. What may be perfectly fine for your friend or teacher may not be fine for you (we all have an inner voice, normally telling us to eat more chocolate and that we're 'not good enough'). Be happy to say no.

Avoid riding with inconsiderate riders or idiots. Choose thoughtful riding companions. Ride in the company of other horses who are not likely to 'set your horse off'. Choose sensible routes out hacking. Choose to ride horses that you feel comfortable with and that go at a pace you can manage. (Okay, so you have this dream of galloping all over the face of the earth, with the wind in your hair, on a wild prancing white stallion – you don't? Oh well, maybe that's just me then.)

3 – Spend as much time as possible around horses

The more you understand the horse's nature and develop an affinity for how horses really are, the easier and more comfortable everything becomes. You may work all week and only get to ride for an hour at the weekend – that's fine. But with a little more time observing these weird and wonderful creatures, you'll soon have horses more under your skin and in your veins.

With plenty of time spent around horses (and remember it costs nothing just to be around) you'll be amazed at how much more understanding and 'horse sense' you'll develop. Whether you ride every day, once a week or less, reach a state where being around horses is second nature. It is a different place in your mind from work, the car, the new contract, relationship hassles, school, driving in heavy traffic, etc.

4 – Increase self-belief by using positive thoughts, speech and action

We have already looked at ways to develop more positive thoughts and how effective they can be in Chapter 10. Tackling nerves and building confidence is a key area where you can put the positive mindpower techniques into practice. If you replace negative thoughts with positive ones, and say positive things instead of negative put-downs, you empower your actions and start to appear more confident and capable. With a little vigilance and effort over your thoughts, words and actions, other people won't believe you when you tell them you are nervous around horses – and the horses won't believe you either!

Watch for when you think and say self-limiting thoughts and phrases such as 'I'm no good at this', 'My seat isn't very secure', 'Horses always run off with me', 'I can't do that.' Try to catch yourself in time and consciously stop any negative words from coming out. They don't need to be said, and they won't help you. If you don't catch the words coming out in time, immediately say the opposite, as a way of cancelling out the negative statement. At first doing this may feel silly and false, and the positive words may not even want to come out of your mouth, but in time it will give you waves of pleasure as your newfound power takes effect. For example, if you were to say, 'My seat isn't very secure', follow it immediately by saying, 'I have a really secure seat in the saddle.'

This might all sound like hard work; it may feel alien at first and part of you will probably not be willing to actually give it a go for a variety of sensible sounding reasons. To overcome any reservations, agree with yourself to try it for, say, just a week and see what happens: that way your mind won't feel as though it is being threatened, forced to change or taken over. If it works for a week, you could say, 'Okay, I'll try it for another week', and so on.

Years ago, every horse of mine used to do so much ridiculous shying that I'd be in the bathroom five times before every hack out, until I realised that the problem was coming from me. In my mind I would be riding along thinking, 'Ooh, I wonder what scary thing is going to jump out the hedge at us next.' Only by replacing those thoughts did my horses quit shying all the time. Fear shown by the herd leader (hopefully you are the herd leader) disturbs the herd followers (hopefully the horse), so that as your mindpower improves your ability to think and act more confidently, horses will go better for you as if by magic, which in turn will make you even more confident.

5 – Become a collector of positive experiences

The more times you ride and get home in one piece, the less evidence and justification your mind has for feeling scared. The more times you get horses to do

Deposit as many safe and successful experiences with horses in your 'confidence bank' as possible.

what you ask them to do, however small and easy the task, the more confident you will become in your own abilities. Put as many safe and successful experiences in your **confidence bank** as possible. Take on very manageable challenges with horses, things you can do easily, and get into the habit of what it feels like for things to go right. It really doesn't matter whether you or anyone else thinks what you are doing with the horse is pathetically easy, your subconscious will still have an enjoyable, positive experience.

6 – Develop body awareness and a seat you can trust

Being nervous starts in the mind, but as soon as we have the slightest 'nervous' thought, our body's reaction is to try and save itself. Unfortunately for riders, horses are particularly perceptive to fear reactions. If we start acting nervously, a horse's natural instinct is either to think its own safety might be threatened, or it starts trying to dominate us. Confident riders usually get better results from horses than more able riders with less confidence, partly because their bodies don't send these messages to the horse.

One of the reasons why riding can be so character-building is the need to overcome our natural reaction to curl up. In reality the safest way to ride is to overcome these instincts and to look ahead, breathe slowly, and not grip, get tense, shout or scream. Easy to say, hey? Here's how...

Body-awareness: Look at the way you move and how you hold your body in everyday life. Do you move in a self-assured or apologetic way? Do you look down a lot, or look confidently ahead? Do you move with quietly confident strides, clumsy clomping or fairy steps? Practise moving and using your body in more centred and 'confident' ways, even if you begin practising privately behind closed doors. How does it make you feel inside to move like a more confident person? In times of fear, see if you can make your body behave as you tell it, and not just do its own thing. Instead of getting tight and curled up, see if you can remain soft, open and flowing, as you have practised beforehand.

Breathing: Horses have the same types of breathing patterns as we do: using mindpower to control your breathing sends the right messages to the horse, messages that he will understand. Take some time to study your breathing. When you are feeling happy, safe and relaxed your breathing is slow, deep, gentle and easy; when you are feeling threatened your breathing will be fast, shallow, sharp and restricted (even to the point of not breathing at all!). As difficult situations start to arise in everyday life, focus your mind on your breathing, guiding it to be slow, deep, soft and easy.

Seat: Having a reliable and balanced seat has to be one of the ultimate ways of feeling secure about your riding. If every time a horse moves in an unexpected direction your balance and seat are disturbed, your mind is quite reasonably informing you that you are not entirely safe. Naturally if your seat is good enough to absorb the horse's unpredictable movements, you are not up the creek without a paddle so often! Developing a good seat takes time, the right tuition and lots of application, but there is no reason why anyone cannot achieve a good classical seat, and the rewards are many.

Taking a series of lessons on the lunge is the ultimate way to improve your seat, with the luxury of not having to control the horse while you ride. (There is more detail on what is required to develop a good seat in Chapter 3, 'True Balance – Standing up with a horse between your legs!')

7 – Live in the present: fear is an inhabitant of the future

Fear is basically founded on what might possibly happen in the future. It follows therefore that if the focus of our attention is in the present, we can reduce some of the limiting effects of our fears.

There are plenty of things to focus on in the present whilst riding:

▶ Is the horse moving straight?

▶ Does he feel the same in both hands or is he leaning more on one rein?

▶ Is his head straight?

▶ Is he going at my tempo?

▶ Is my seat soft on his back?

▶ Is my back and neck soft?

▶ Am I looking where I want to go?

▶ Are my legs hanging down nicely or gripping?

▶ What is my breathing doing?

▶ Am I smiling or frowning?

▶ Can I feel each of his footfalls in turn?

▶ Is he light off my leg?

All of these details and more will not only help you to live in the present moment, but improve your riding and communication with the horse.

Ask yourself: 'What am I focusing on right now?'

The opposite is to ride along thinking 'Oh God, what if...' or 'I hope the horse doesn't do such and such,' and not giving the horse or yourself anything else to think about other than the imaginary horror of scary possibilities.

Of course, one of the arts of effective horsemanship is being able to diffuse problems before they happen, but that can still be done whilst the main focus of your mind/body and the horse's mind are still in the present. You can achieve this by having two minds: one mind is in the present, riding the horse and controlling your body, and the other is a secret mind that quietly keeps 'an eye out' for possible trouble and whose thoughts are hidden from the horse and from your body. It may sound like a pretty whacky idea, but it is actually quite simple to do ... and it works!

8 – Visualisation

Visualisations are going on in our minds the whole time like internal movies, and not all of them are helpful. Instead of our imagination running the personal movie projector we can consciously run it ourselves, and decide to see programmes that will bring about success, confidence and self-belief, rather than the opposite.

What we visualise very often comes about and also sets off reactions in our body and mind.

So if we visualise something scary, guess how we're going to feel ... that's right, scared.

If we visualise ourselves being a brilliant rider, guess what we'll be! (See Chapter 13, 'Visualisation and imagination'.)

9 – Constantly remind yourself that you are riding for fun

That may sound pretty obvious, but it is amazing how easy it is to forget that riding is primarily a fun pastime. Why else would anyone want to do it?

If you are having fun you're on the right track. On a scale of one to ten, where one is blind panic and ten is ecstasy, if the fun level drops below five, move the goal-posts, change the situation, lower the demands upon yourself or the horse, and get back to enjoying your riding.

Some people have fun being scared, and it is true to say that the unpredictability of horses adds a certain spice to riding, but it is all a matter of degree. Know at what point the excitement ends and the struggle kicks in. What is fun for one person may be a fate worse than death for someone else. Recognise where the fun lies for you – you can always change your mind and take on more challenges at a later date.

Ask yourself honestly if you are a 'fear junkie', someone who is hooked on the idea of being scared. If the answer is 'yes', ask yourself 'why?'

10. – Anchors

Anchors are messages, phrases or thoughts you can call upon to regain control of your body and your state of mind in times of stress or panic. Everyone will have different anchors, but whatever you choose as your anchor should be easy for you to call up and have an emotionally calming or empowering effect on you.

Your anchor may be to think about slow breathing, it may be to see yourself as a great rider, an image of a role model, it may be a word or phrase such as 'looking ahead', 'calm, calm, calm', or 'feeling great'. I have even whistled or sung silly songs in times of extremis. It is hard to hold your breath or have a horrified and tense look on your face if you are whistling or singing, 'Happy, happy, happy talk, talk about things we like to do...' from the musical *South Pacific*!

A 'step-by-step to confidence' exercise

If you feel apprehensive about riding, but want to do it anyway, follow these steps one at a time, and only move on to the next step when you feel totally at ease with the step you're on. This exercise can help with 'jumpy' horses as well as 'jumpy' riders. The more time you take over this exercise, the more effective and solid are the results.

▶ **STEP 1**: Lead the horse around (from the ground) with some slack in the reins and ask for a few halts. Whatever the horse does with you on the ground he'll do the same in the saddle, so if you can't stop him nicely now, you won't be able to when you ride.

▶ **STEP 2**: If the horse stands still to be mounted, mount up somewhere safe. If the horse won't stand totally still don't get on, wait patiently until he does, or get expert help: he's not physically or mentally ready to be ridden. Once you are on board, just sit in the saddle in halt until you get bored (it could be a minute or two hours).

▶ **STEP 3**: Now that you're bored, you'll want to do a bit more, so ask the horse to walk in circles of about 10 metres, alternating right then left, with the reins as long as possible. Do that until you get bored (could be two minutes, but no longer than fifteen minutes in any one session, for the sake of the horse's leg joints).

▶ **STEP 4**: Repeat Step 3 until you are bored enough to want to do more. Maybe now you could try some straight lines and bigger circles.

▶ **STEP 5**: As you get bored with each step, go on to do a little more, until you reach ...

▶ **STEP 6,000,000**: Go round Badminton cross-country course with no stirrups!

Things to do...

1. Have faith.

2. Remember that riding is for fun and pleasure, nothing else!

3. Try all of my ten tips for building confidence and conquering nerves.

4. Remember you are not alone: everyone could do with wearing a pair of brown jodhpurs at some point in their riding career! (Did I really write that? Oops!)

5. Be patient with yourself and take as long as it takes to build confidence.

Quick reference...

Build up confidence slowly but surely: don't compare yourself to others: don't do things that scare you: you **CAN** do it: be kind to yourself: have as many good and easy experiences with horses as you can.

Chapter 15

Beyond the mind: the state of true 'being' with horses

Have you ever had those moments with a horse when time seems to stand still? You feel totally uplifted by the experience. It is as though you are floating on air. You feel completely connected with the horse and your surroundings and totally at peace inside yourself. Everything you try to do with the horse happens easily and simply, as though the horse were part of your inner self, reading your mind and carrying out your wishes even before you have asked.

This is what riding is really about. You and the horse are transformed into one centaur-like creature, and are transported together into a different state, a state of pure 'being'.

If those feelings are familiar to you, then you would no doubt like to reproduce them more often. If you have never felt that experience, you will no doubt want to feel it. Part of you intuitively knows of its existence already, and is looking for that experience through communion with that most magical of creatures, the horse.

You do not have to be an advanced rider to experience these moments with a horse. In fact, in some ways it can be more difficult for advanced riders, because they often have so many more objectives, standards and expectations of their riding.

Imagine you're a horse...

You form deep bonds; you love your friends and family.

> Remember: the horse is always fully present. Can you join him there?

How do we create a state of true 'being' with the horse?

Most of this book is about putting in place the necessary ingredients by which to bring about a state of 'being' with horses. Actually we can't create these moments, but what we can do is to create the conditions for them to come about, and then allow them to happen. Let's look at what those conditions are:

▶ You sit in union with the horse. Once your body is in true balance, absolutely vertical, it can be 'quiet' and still, i.e. not using muscle tension to defy gravity, grip or help you to stay on the horse.

▶ Focus on your breath, allowing it to filter gently through your whole body and down into the body of the horse.

▶ Your aids become very quiet, almost non-existent, so the horse listens more carefully and your body has even more chance to be still.

▶ You let ambition fall away from your mind but you still hold an intention and ride accurately to where you wish. At the same time you don't judge how it is going, or get annoyed if things aren't perfect.

▶ You lock onto the metronome in your head, and the horse joins you in that regular, hypnotic tempo.

▶ You 'feel' the horse. You 'feel' where he is mentally, but also feel his body and every movement and footfall. His feet become your feet, his spine becomes your spine.

▶ You gaze softly into the middle distance.

▶ You quieten your inner voice (thoughts) and your outer voice (talking). You cannot feel enough when either voice is chattering. Become a 'horse listener' in every moment that you ride, by being quiet yourself.

▶ You see what comes along.

▶ You establish the riding in an environment that is 'safe' for both you and the horse. Do exercises that are within the capabilities of both you and the horse.

▶ You let go of doubts and worries. You lower your expectations.

▶ You enjoy the moment, then enjoy the next moment, then the next, etc.

▶ You keep a broad focus, not concentrating on one detail or another; you just let everything that needs to come to your attention quietly be known to you.

► You allow yourself to 'be' with the horse, not against him. You let him know you are there. You focus on the communication between the two of you. You focus on what you are feeling, rather than what you are thinking.

► You give up **trying**, and you give up **doing**. You just ride by **being**.

Developing awareness and 'feel'

To ride really well requires a refined degree of focused attention on what the horse is doing from moment to moment, with his mind and body, and also what we are doing with our bodies. As soon as we start pressing for results, we don't have enough mental awareness on the present to 'listen' to all the aspects of what is happening between the horse and ourselves.

Many novice riders, and some more advanced riders, may wonder exactly what they are supposed to be listening to from moment to moment, but as soon as you still your mind and quieten your body, you start to develop awareness. You may start to feel:

► The horse's feet touch the ground one by one.

► His back moving side to side.

► One side of his mouth being softer than the other.

► The energy coming up along his spine.

► The horse putting uneven weight onto one shoulder or the other.

► Tension in his back or neck

► The horse's mind start to wander, etc.

You may also start to feel:

► Your shoulders being tight, or tension in your neck, back or jaw.

► You may become aware of uneven pressure on the stirrups or that you are sitting twisted or slightly over to one side.

► You may feel the horse shifting your seat over to one side or the other.

► You may start to notice anxiety creeping into your mind as you prepare for a canter transition.

► You may feel yourself start to fill with dread as you approach a 7ft 2ins fence (and why not, I say!) etc.

Whatever you are doing or wherever you are with the horse, be there **totally**.

All these things and more start to enter your awareness as you become more 'present-moment' focused.

The benefit of developing this awareness is huge. As your awareness develops, you are acquiring that mysterious thing called 'feel'. Once you know what is happening to you or the horse from moment to moment, you are empowered to respond by doing just the right thing at the right moment:

This is where real riding starts.

And you do not have to be a master to begin to experience it. You simply have to **BE** there, in the present moment, quietly listening to yourself and to the horse, responding in the right, subtle way at the right time and waiting for a response from the horse.

Things to do...

1. Follow the steps described above and see where they take you.

2. Notice what you are doing when you have a wonderful experience with a horse, and more importantly, recall what you did just before the experience, so that you can recreate it some other time.

3. Develop your sense of 'feel'. This is what riding is really about, and you don't have to be an expert to enjoy the odd moment of 'divine sensation', as Xenophon described it 2500 years ago.

4. Fantastic riding experiences begin with one or two exquisite moments, and then they go. Don't lose heart. Gradually you will have longer and more frequent moments of riding in a state of true 'being' with the horse.

Part 4

Partnership Work

Real riding is all about partnership: it is the essential ingredient that brings about those moments where you and the horse are one, his spine is your spine, his feet are your feet, the same breeze blows through his mane as across your face, time and the world disappear and you lose yourself in being 'as one'.

Partnership means you and the horse working together on the same team. Yes, you decide what you are doing and the horse follows through with your requests, but it comes from a place of mutual respect and unity. Using strength or domination to force horses to do what we want may look impressive, but it is not a part of true excellence, nor is it as deeply satisfying as riding from a place of togetherness with the horse.

This state of partnership grows and is cultivated by working **with** the horse's nature, being in control of yourself physically, mentally and emotionally, and judiciously using tried and tested training techniques appropriately to develop rapport, to take your horse and rider communication to a whole new level and to enhance performance. **Partnership work is the source of the heart and soul of riding.**

Chapter 16

The three paces

Walk, trot and canter are pretty much what riding is all about. There are particular benefits and difficulties unique to riding in each of the three paces, and it is by no means easy to master all of the ins and outs of walk, trot and canter ... so let's have a look.

Some thoughts on the walk

Riding in walk gives the rider plenty of time to think and feel what is going on.

Being ridden in walk gives the horse plenty of time to think about what it is supposed to be doing, or what the rider is asking.

Practising turns and learning lateral movements (sideways stuff) can best be learned at the walk, for both horse and rider.

Horses don't normally get too fizzy or hyped-up in walk – it is not very exciting.

Walking small school figures (circles, serpentines, figure of eights) can be a good way to settle an inattentive horse.

Walk is a nice, un-bouncy pace in which to spend time working on your riding position, posture, and relaxation of body and mind in preparation for the faster and more unseating gaits.

Spending plenty of time in walk is a gentle way to warm the horse up, especially if he's been stabled. Gradually making more demanding and complex patterns in walk helps to get the horse soft and well loosened.

Learning to feel the four individual footfalls of walk is a great exercise for the rider. The sway of the horse's back and belly from side to side at walk helps the rider to feel the hind feet. The hind-leg movement can be felt through the rider's seat and lower leg.

The movement of the forelegs can be felt through the rider's **relaxed** knees.

Once the rider can easily feel the footfalls of the forelegs in walk (without looking!) it is easy to apply the same feel of the forelegs in canter. With practice the rider then has no trouble whatsoever in feeling which canter lead the horse is on – without looking down to check.

Walking on a long rein is a way of rewarding the horse for something well done or strenuous. It is also an important way to start and finish the ridden work.

Some thoughts on the trot

It is perhaps too often said that the trot is **the** pace in which to **work** the horse. Consequently the world seems to be full of riders and horses grinding round and round in a brisk working trot, because 'that's what one is supposed to do'.

There are dozens of variations in trot pace and feel, not just collected, working and extended. The more 'trot feels' the rider can imagine, the more 'trot feels' the horse can offer up.

Trot is a symmetrical gait, which means it can be easier to work the whole horse more evenly than in walk or canter.

When the horse is mentally and emotionally 'with' the rider, the trot pace becomes smoother and easier to sit to. A married couple doing ballroom-dancing won't flow too well if they've just had a blazing row, whereas a couple who are feeling helplessly in love and emotionally 'together' will still produce some kind of magic and unity, even if they have four left feet between them!

Always look for rhythm in the trot. Have the metronome ticking away like clockwork in your head. That's where the rhythm comes from. It doesn't falter or alter: It. Just. Stays. The. Same. No. Speeding. Up. And. No. Slowing. Down. Just. 1-2-3-4 , 1-2-3-4, 1-2-3-4. Keep that metronome ticking in your head

Ask yourself: 'What would be the most effective thing for me and this horse to do right now?'

and the horse will start fitting in with it.

The trot doesn't have to be fast to have impulsion – the ultimately impulsive trot is the piaffe, in which the horse goes nowhere whatsoever. Horses often try to trot faster to save themselves the effort of using their hindquarters, which is where the impulsion comes from.

Practise sitting trot at a steady pace. It's no use trying to sit to a bouncy, lumpy, fast trot like a desperado on top of a furry pogo-stick. Trying to ride a bigger trot than you're really ready for can't be much fun for the horse's back either.

In sitting trot, look ahead, feel the point of balance going forwards, and focus your mind on your seat – that is, the area where you and the horse are joined together through the saddle. Soften, soften, soften your seat and waist and roll with the motion of the horse's back. Remind yourself to look ahead, again and again.

Practise sitting trot for a few really quality strides, and then come back to walk or rising trot, recompose yourself and take sitting trot again.

It's a shame rising trot is called 'rising' trot. Actually, if you just go up and down you instantly get left behind the horse's forward movement, your lower legs go forwards and it all goes a bit 'pear-shaped'. The movement of the rider's seat is more forwards then down, then forwards then down, etc.; that way the rider keeps up with the horse's forward movement.

In rising trot, carry your hands wide enough apart so that they don't get in the way of your hips coming forwards during the 'rise'.

Many people's hands go up and down with the rise of their body. To get around this, THINK of your elbows being left behind you as you rise. Don't actually do it, just THINK it. Allow the arms to hang freely from the shoulder, rather than being fixed like they're welded onto your body.

To help with the freedom and forward feeling of your rising trot, practise standing up in the stirrups, first in halt, then walk, and then trot. This will help to get the hips well forwards. You almost feel as though your hips need to go so far forward you're sitting on his ears!

Let the ankles, knees and hips be soft for rising and sitting trot.

During the 'rise' phase of the rising trot, feel as if you are leaving your feet behind you.

See if you can trot without doing 'leg, leg, leg' aids with every stride. Set

the trot up, then let it happen as much as possible.

Trot a while with long reins, so that the horse has to find his own balance, instead of you holding his head. This will help you find your balance without his head holding you too.

Remember trotting should be FUN and PLEASURABLE!.

You decide on the tempo (speed) of the trot. Notice if the horse gradually starts to alter the tempo, and remind him what your idea of the tempo is.

Use smaller circles occasionally to rebalance the horse's trot.

In sitting trot, a large amount of the horse's movement needs to be absorbed in the rider's lower back and waist. The more movement that can be absorbed there, the less the hands, shoulders and head need to 'bob' about. To do this means not pushing too actively with your seat, back or legs. You need to be poised and yet as soft and relaxed as possible, without losing your 'form' and turning into a jelly-like blob.

The quality of the preparation and transition into trot has a huge effect on the quality of the trot itself. A sloppy transition leaves loads of mess to be cleaned up once the trot is underway, which makes things far more difficult than making good preparations beforehand.

Rein-back has the same sequence of legs as the trot.

Some thoughts on the canter

Canter has an in-built difficulty in the horse's mind: canter is the horse's natural means of escaping from being eaten for dinner. It is the instinctive 'flight' pace.

> Canter does not necessarily mean faster; it is just the horse's legs moving in a different order.

If the horse isn't settled in his mind, it may not be the best moment to ask for canter.

There are lots of different combinations of aids to get into canter: some horses need a different combination of the aids: experiment!

Think 'CANTER', ask for a slight flexion of the horse's head to the 'inside', place your outside leg slightly behind the girth (left leg if you are going round to the right, i.e. clockwise) and use your inside leg actively on the girth. Be 'willing' to canter with your body when the horse strikes off, but don't force, push or start cantering before the horse does. Wait for the horse to 'take you' on into the canter.

To get into canter, you set it up and allow it to happen, instead of trying to **make** the horse canter.

Looking ahead and not at the horse is particularly effective in canter. Looking down puts extra weight on the horse's shoulders (remember, even your eyeballs weigh 20 stone on a horse) and makes it more difficult for him to pick himself up into the canter.

Looking down to 'check' what canter lead you are on is a very common habit, but quite unnecessary. The other unnecessary, and often inaccurate, way that people tell which canter lead they are on is 'if he feels uncomfortable I know it's the right lead and if it feels comfortable I know it must be left lead!' I know, I've been there and done that myself.

The true way to tell which lead you are on is to feel it, and until you can feel it, it is very frustrating, so you revert back to the previous methods. Instead of that, learn to feel the front legs in walk, as above, then apply the same feeling in canter. Hey presto, you've got it!

Canter doesn't necessarily mean going any faster than trot or walk. Canter is simply about the horse's legs going in a different order. Horses can be trained to canter on the spot, or even backwards!

If the horse needs more impulsion or interest whilst in walk or trot, practise a few transitions into canter and back down again. This may help to increase the amount of energy the horse gives to you.

Don't surprise the horse into canter by going 'trot, trot, trot, trot, trot, trot, **CANTER**!' Try to invite or ease him into it. Ask the horse to canter, don't kick him to canter. Use very quiet aids and wait for a result.

If the trot speeds up to get into canter, slow it again, and ask for canter again next time round.

People often don't canter for long enough. If the horse is fairly fit and it is a safe situation, try cantering for, say five, ten or fifteen minutes without stopping. You and the horse should start to get more relaxed and into a rhythm. It may also get you a little bit fitter!

Sometimes it helps to do the opposite of cantering for a long time: try cantering for exactly fifteen strides, then ten, then five strides, walking in between each canter. This is a good way to help the horse to stay in balance and also avoids the rider becoming overly tense.

See if you can smile whilst going into canter, and continue smiling whilst cantering around, and coming back down to walk.

Remember to keep breathing while you canter. Try breathing out as you go into canter.

The deeper and more relaxed your legs are, the more balanced and steadily the horse can canter.

Let your hips rock loosely back and forth, allowing your body above the waist to remain upright, i.e. not tipping back or leaning forwards.

On a safe horse, try doing some canter with no rein contact, e.g. on the lunge.

Maintain a nice, soft, correct riding position in canter, hopefully as correct as the one you have established in walk, and everything should become much easier. People often go into all sorts of contortions in canter.

Don't push hard with the seat. Be quiet and soft.

Canter the horse when you and him are physically and mentally 'ready' to canter.

Feeling the three paces

> When you're on a horse, his feet are your connection with the ground.

As we have seen already, when you are on the horse, his legs are your legs. Also, to give the aids at the right moment in his stride requires us to be able to know at any given moment what the horse is doing with his legs. Since we spend most of our lives on only two legs, it can be an interesting challenge for us to learn this.

Although learning to feel the horse's feet may at first sound a bit technical, difficult or boring, actually it can be good fun and will start to transform your riding and your 'feel'.

> This stuff is so important that there is nearly always a series of photos or drawings of the horse's leg sequence near the beginning of every riding book, but it is something we normally skip straight past.

On your knees!

The best way to begin is on your hands and knees on the carpet. Start by going up and down the room in trot (alternate diagonals, that's easy).

Then, still on your hands and knees, proceed to a specific canter lead. Let's

> If riding is
> pleasurable for you,
> look for ways in
> which your riding
> can be pleasurable
> for the horse.

start with the left lead: so it's right hind, right fore and left hind together, and then left fore on its own. Phewee! Try that again. Now reverse the leg sequence and try right lead without my help. (Cantering doesn't mean you have to go fast, and you can forget the moment of suspension, unless you are adept at yogic flying!)

Now in the walk: right fore, left hind, left fore, right hind – that's complicated.

What about rein back? It is the trot sequence backwards.

Try some lateral work and let the feel of it soak into your body.

What about trying a flying change as you go past the armchair? How much fun can you have?

Practise the above paces on your hands and knees until they become easy or your knees get too sore: I guarantee it will improve your riding.

On the horse!

In walk and then trot, sit with your legs and seat as relaxed as possible, look ahead and flow with the movement of the horse's back. Can you feel the saddle, the horse's back, his belly and your seat swing gently from side to side? As his belly and your leg go inwards, e.g. on the right, he is starting a step with his right hind leg, that is the best moment to give a leg aid with the right leg. When the same thing happens on the left, he is picking up his left hind leg.

Call out left, right, left, right as you feel each hind leg leaving the ground. Have someone on the ground tell you when you are correct. At first this stuff might strain your brain, but in the long run it will pay huge dividends. With a little practice you'll be tickled pink at how easy this is, and pretty soon it will filter down into your subconscious and become a part of your 'feel'.

To feel the forelegs is easier: focus on the feeling of movement through your knees.

Things to do...

1. Practise the exercise of walking, trotting and cantering on your hands and knees until the feel of the three paces becomes second nature to you.

2. Practise feeling the sequence of the horse's feet in all three paces when you ride.

3. In a safe environment, ride with your eyes closed and feel the way the horse's back moves in each of the three paces. You could do this more easily on the lunge.

4. Ride in all three paces, rather than sticking mostly to one or two. Use the benefits of each pace for your riding and your horse's training progress.

Quick reference...

All three paces have their own particular benefits and challenges; familiarity with each pace is essential; walk gives you lots of time and lowers energy levels; trot is a symmetrical gait, useful for much of the work; canter is more exciting for the horse and can be used for more energy; the horse's feet are your feet whilst you ride.

Chapter 17

School figures: how and why never to find them boring!

'Oh, my horse hates schooling.' Ever heard that before? What about this one: 'Oh, riding in the school is so boring'? Or how about: 'What is the point of riding in the school at all once you've learned enough to ride, control a horse and not fall off?'

For the rider

Riding in the school is helpful for riders with any level of experience. It gives the rider the chance to improve their balance, the quality of their position on the horse, their safety, effectiveness and communication skills. Riding in the school enables the rider to learn to 'feel' more of what the horse is doing, or about to do, underneath them. Riding in the school helps the rider to develop some finesse in their riding. The more skilful and knowledgeable the rider becomes, the more pleasure and sense of satisfaction they can derive from riding.

For the horse

Riding in the school helps the horse to learn to readjust its balance under the unnatural weight of a rider. It is also a good environment in which to learn and develop responses to the common language of the 'aids', which do need to be learned by the horse, as well as by the rider. Schoolwork done well can give the horse an increased level of suppleness and a feeling of physical well-being, and

> Make all your decisions, aids and communication crystal clear.

it can be interesting and mentally stimulating for the horse. It can be like a 'horsy yoga' session.

What constitutes a school figure?

A school figure is an accurate geometric shape of a particular size, on which you decide to ride. Examples may include circles, serpentines, half-circles and figures of eight, but not potato, banana or any patterns reminiscent of the 'Chaos Theory!'

What is the basic purpose of school figures?

Riding a school figure gives you and the horse a plan to follow, without which you'd just be doodling around at random. The fact that you have a plan to work to means you can tell how things are going by how closely you and the horse have managed to stick to the plan, or not, as the case may be!

How do school figures help the horse?

Riding school figures with a curve in them, e.g. a circle, is an excellent way to make the horse physically better able to carry the weight of a rider. The horse's front legs and back legs should always follow exactly the line of the circle, and in learning to do this well, the horse will build up the strength of his body and become more supple. It may be a surprise to learn that horses need to be made even stronger and suppler than they are naturally in order to carry a rider.

Oh, and by the way, riding school figures accurately goes a long way towards getting horses on the bit.

Do school figures have any other benefits?

Riding accurate school figures provides a mental focus for the horse and the rider, which helps the two beings to be more harmonious, more calm and collected (mentally and therefore physically), less distracted by outside influences and better able to concentrate on each other.

How should I start a schooling session?

Begin every school session on a totally long rein, if possible, and ride around the outside track of the school each way a couple of times to help the horse loosen up his body. End each schooling session this way too, especially if the horse has worked hard, is sweating or breathing heavily.

What can I do not to get bored just riding round in circles?

If you are 'feeling' the horse's body, listening to his body with your body and responding moment by moment to what the horse is doing underneath you on a circle, you won't have time to be bored. Every step, every moment and every stride on a circle is likely to be telling you something, and you need to respond to that something in the appropriate way.

What should I feel for when I do school figures?

Here are some ideas of what to feel for, and how to respond:

> Ask yourself: 'Which side of the horse is his stiff side?'

► Can you feel whether it is you or the horse that is deciding on the exact speed at which you are both travelling? Decide on your speed with your mind and body and the horse must follow you. Ride with an imaginary metronome ticking accurately in your head (see also the advice on timing in Chapter 16). Horses will rush, go sluggish or not keep a regular speed in order to avoid doing good schoolwork.

► Is the horse softer in one of your hands and stiffer in the other, or carrying his head more to the left or right? Once you have noticed which side of his mouth the horse is stiffer on, try to play and vibrate the rein a little on that side, until the reins become even. What it usually means when the horse is stiffer on one rein is that his hind leg on that side is not as active and supple as the side where his mouth is soft. This is important. Try to keep in mind that you need to activate his stiff hind leg a little ... without him speeding up! Now are you still bored?

► Can you feel whether the horse is carrying his hindquarters a little to the left or to the right? It is quite rare for a horse to be naturally straight. You may find it easier to feel this at first on the straight, long side. Try correcting his quarters by slightly turning your hips the way you want his hips to be, e.g. if he carries his quarters to the left, gently bring your left hip back a little and your right hip forward, whilst not tipping your weight to one side, keeping his head straight and not letting him alter the tempo! Still bored?

Imagine you're a horse...

You are stimulated mentally, physically and emotionally by doing interesting work with a sensitive rider.

The aim is to get the horse to carry himself evenly over all four legs, not favouring one more than another.

▶ As you go round a circle it is pretty likely that the horse will 'fall' onto one shoulder or the other – can you feel which shoulder? Most likely it is the shoulder opposite to the way his head and neck are facing, i.e. if he is going around to the right, with his head and neck bent to the right, he will be falling onto his left shoulder.

If the horse is dropping more weight on one shoulder, his energies are escaping out of that shoulder. He is not carrying himself as well as he could, nor is he carrying you as well as he could, and you are not in control of that quarter of his body. To correct it, decrease the bend of his head a little, and feel a bit more rein on the side of the 'falling out' shoulder. Repeat this feel on the rein of the falling-out shoulder as necessary, until the horse carries both shoulders the same – without him doing any of the things mentioned in 1, 2 or 3 above. (Tricky, eh?) Still bored, or just over-loaded with 'stuff' to do?

▶ Horses often push their ribs into the circle slightly at the girth, therefore not truly coming round the circle, and avoiding working their hind legs properly. Can you feel whether the horse responds lightly to your inside leg, or just seems to be unresponsive to it? If he isn't truly responsive to a light inside leg, this is what to do: momentarily feel a bit more on the outside rein and touch lightly with the leg, making the leg slightly longer and deeper as you ask, rather than gripping, kicking, squeezing or drawing it up. Follow this leg aid an instant later with a touch of the schooling stick just behind the leg if you need to. Do this every time you feel the horse being dull to the lightest touch of the inside leg on the circle, but remember not to let any of the things in 1, 2, 3 or 4 above happen as a result. Still bored, or just confused and exhausted?!

▶ Take a break every few minutes or you will fry your brains and wear out the horse.

Does the horse get bored doing school figures?

As long as you make schoolwork interesting and find it interesting yourself, horses can get really interested too. The danger with schoolwork is that you start finding it too absorbing, get carried away with it, forget how long you've been there, and exhaust the poor horse.

How long should I do school figures for?

This depends on the horse's level of training and fitness, how he feels that day and how well you are both working. Always try to strike a balance, and be aware of how the horse feels.

Generally speaking, ride school figures for less time than you think, to avoid unnecessary wear and tear. Four hours of hacking can be less wearing on a horse's body than thirty minutes in the school. As a guide, the Spanish Riding School of Vienna generally works each horse for only a thirty-minute session, including a warm-up, cool down and rests in between.

How do I know what school figure to do at any given moment?

> Ask yourself: 'What school figure would most serve me and the horse right now?' If the horse is rushing or needs collecting, use smaller circles, if he needs to stretch or go forwards more, use large figures and straight lines.

This is good question, and it depends on the stage of training. The thing to remember is that the smaller the school figure, the harder it is on the horse, so a 10m circle is more demanding than a 20m circle, etc. Remember that it is good to change the rein more often than you think. Two to four circles on the right and it is probably time to change the rein, and go around to the left. Since smaller figures are more demanding for the horse, start each session doing larger, easier figures and gradually increase the demands by doing some smaller figures.

Watch for the horse anticipating school figures. If you feel this, do figures that he is not anticipating. It is up to you to decide what you do, where and when. It helps to make it interesting for the horse and keeps him guessing.

Integrate plenty of transitions into your schoolwork, from one pace to another or from extended to collected within each pace. Gradually you will also increase the amount of lateral work too.

Things to do...

1. Start to get interested in school figures. Think of them like the scales in music. The better you are at them, the more music you and the horse can make together.

2. Always try to be as accurate as possible. Put some markers or cones out to mark exact figures.

3. Rest a lot. Look at the time and make sure you don't overdo it.

4. Watch as many brilliant riders schooling as you can. Ask yourself why they may have decided to do a particular school figure at any given time. They should have a reason for their choice.

5. Keep smiling. School figures are absorbing but should still be fun.

Quick reference...

School figures are great for the horse and the rider; if you listen and respond to the horse, they are never boring; there is lots of fine detail involved; school riding can be very interesting, physically and mentally for horse and rider.

Chapter 18

To be or not to be 'on the bit'

There is a lot of talk about being 'on the bit' and a lot of different ideas about exactly what it means and how essential it is. In essence, being on the bit means that the horse's maximum energies and forces are 'collected' into a controllable form. It is basically the same as when a horse naturally gathers these energies together himself, in order to fight, escape, play or pose about. Watch horses practising 'horse-play' in the field together to see them truly on the bit, and not a rider or bridle in sight!

Putting the horse correctly on the bit helps the horse to be better able to carry the weight of the rider. In the same way that an arched bridge has a natural strength, the horse's body has more athletic weight-carrying ability when it forms the arched shape by being on the bit.

Being on the bit is not an end goal; it should just be part of an on-going process. It should happen in the course of correct training almost as a by-product of lining the horse up, tuning him to the aids, building and developing suppleness and muscles over a period of months and years.

What is 'on the bit' and what is not 'on the bit'

A horse that is on the bit looks and feels light, soft, flowing and powerful in his movement; he has his head at such an angle that his face is just ahead of the vertical; his neck is reaching forward and up so that the poll (just behind the ears) is the highest point; his whole shape from nose to tail forms a kind of arch, and he is actively flexing and 'using' his hind legs. The overall appearance

An interesting thing about riding different horses on the bit is that they tend to feel similar to each other, as opposed to when they go around in their own individual, uncollected way.

of a horse that is truly on the bit should be eye-catching and one of beauty.

It is possible to see horses worked on the bit with too much force. Rather than appearing to be more beautiful they have the look of a slightly sad, somewhat over-worked, repressed servant.

Admittedly, horses do look nicer when they have their neck arched and their head in, but it is important to note from the above that this is only part of the story. Having the head in doesn't necessarily mean the horse is working properly at all.

The phrase 'on the bit' is misleading because it tends to make us focus on what is happening in the front end of the horse, instead of concentrating on feeling and looking at what is happening underneath our seat and in the hindquarters, where the true 'coming together' happens.

Horses generally feel better underneath you when they are on the bit. The contact becomes more consistent and lighter, the horse's trot and canter become smoother and easier to sit to, his rhythm becomes more regular, his back feels more 'expensively' sprung and the aids seem to work more easily. Taking a totally lumpy, un-together horse and getting it to go truly on the bit feels something like taking an old budget car and turning it into a Rolls Royce (well, OK, maybe a BMW at least). Pretty amazing stuff really!

Don't forget the horse's mind

To me, being truly on the bit means that the horse is not only yielding to the rider with his body, but he is also 'accepting' with his mind, as if he is saying, 'Yes, I am with you and happy to do this.' This is a really important part of having a horse work properly for you. The mind and body of the horse are intrinsically linked, so if he feels like being a plank, his body will be a plank; similarly if he feels like having a compliant and accepting attitude, his body will feel that way too. Unless the horse's mind is with you, riding him on the bit will require more force to achieve and maintain. It will feel a little like fools' gold instead of the genuine 22ct stuff! Once you've felt the real thing, you won't be happy with cheap imitations.

What kinds of things are possible when a horse is not on the bit?

► Is it possible to trot? Yes

► Is it possible to canter? Yes

► Is it possible to jump? Yes

► Is it possible to stop? Yes

► Is it possible to go hacking? Yes

► Is it possible to ride safely? Yes

► Is it possible to be 'in control'? Yes

► Is it possible to use the horse as a means of transport? Yes

► Is it possible to do collected work? No, not really

► Is it possible to be communicating with the horse? Yes definitely

► Is it possible to win a dressage competition? Shouldn't be!

► Is it possible to have a good time? Yes

I do all the above things 'not on the bit' some days with my horses, in order to keep them feeling mentally interested and physically relaxed.

Just to break up the routine of how things are done, it sometimes benefits both the rider and the horse to ride a whole session with as little or no collection as possible. Some people may foam at the mouth in disagreement with this idea, but I bet most horses wouldn't mind. Play around with it; try a more 'Western' approach for a session or two. See how responsive you can get the horse with little or no collection. See if it makes him more responsive and improves his attitude when you go back to looking for more 'collected' work.

(Safety is obviously a consideration; so don't do anything that might involve taking unnecessary risks.)

If you were a horse, how much would you want to be on the bit, and how would you like to be put on the bit?

This is where things can get a little tricky because some people believe that horses should be on the bit the whole time, but I think that the majority of horses would wholeheartedly disagree. Being on the bit requires a lot of effort on the part of the horse, and for his sake it is therefore not ideal to have him on the bit the whole time when you ride. It is a lot to ask of the horse that he goes on the bit within the first few moments or so that he is ridden, while his

> If I were a horse my heart would sink at hearing the instruction, 'get him between hand and leg'. In essence, that is what being on the bit is about, but the expression leads to a lot of forced entrapment, lots of determination from the rider, lots of compressing of horses' bodies and lots of force. As a horse, I certainly wouldn't want someone to get me into a brisk working trot, set a good, firm rein contact and then 'push' all 500kgs of me up to the bridle with a strong back, seat and leg, leg, legs. No thanks!

Imagine you're a horse...

You are not at all dumb (just misunderstood sometimes).

body is not warmed up enough. The more you can do with a horse on a light or loose rein the better. That way, when he works on the bit, you are more likely to have a willing partner than a repressed servant who just thinks, 'Oh-oh, here we go again doing these demanding aerobics.' Done with discretion, riding on the bit can give the horse a very pleasant feeling, almost as though he has been to an equine yoga class. That is what **you** want to be looking for on the horse's behalf.

Ideas to put horses on the bit with harmony

► Have a light contact with the horse's mouth (see Chapter 6 on contact). If the horse throws his head up or opens his mouth, the contact may well be too hard; if the reins don't look straight, like two sticks, the contact is possibly too light or inconsistent.

► Have a soft, allowing seat. Sit upright, but without stiffness. Have soft shoulders, neck, hands, arms, wrists and waist. Feel for your point of balance all the time.

► Make sure your thighs are lying softly on the saddle and not gripping, as this will make it difficult for the horse to lift his back and open his ribs. Look at the 'breathing trick' (in Chapter 3) where you breathe in through your hands and out through your seat/heels/thighs etc. and apply it to your seat and thighs.

► Work mostly at a fairly steady tempo.

► Have your lower leg lightly on the horse's sides so that he maintains the tempo and goes willingly forwards.

► If the horse is really dead to the legs, tap him with a schooling stick rather than using stronger legs, but make sure you don't jerk on the reins with the stick hand. Keep allowing the horse to flow forwards. **Strong legs actually make it more difficult for the horse to use himself properly as they restrict the freedom of his body.**

► Make sure the horse's head is straight and the contact is the same in each rein. If the contact is firmer in one rein, use the leg on that side and vibrate that rein in your fingers until he softens that side of his mouth.

► Try halting for a few seconds, keeping the rein and leg contact lightly there, then walk six, eight or ten more strides and halt again. Do this a few times.

▶ **Any time the horse softens, even by the slightest amount, you must immediately soften yourself a little too.This is the single most important factor in this approach. THE HORSE NEEDS TO KNOW THAT <u>YOU KNOW</u> THAT HE HAS GIVEN TO YOU! The softening you give to him may be so tiny that it is little more than a thought, or a slight physical giving of the reins if you feel the horse needs a clearer message that he has done right.**

▶ Try turning a few accurate 10m, 8m or 6m circles in walk without bending the horse's head too much to the inside. Try to turn keeping both reins the same length and both hands next to each other as a pair.

▶ Check through the second tip given above every few strides!

▶ Check out Chapter 17 on school figures. Riding accurate school figures with a sound knowledge of why you are doing them and what you want to feel is a huge key to getting horses to work correctly. When school figures are done well, it is almost as though the horse comes on the bit all by himself.

▶ **The main thing is that you are don't force the horse on to the bit, but set things up and wait for him to give the right response.**

> Remember to set things up and wait.

▶ Practise spiralling in from a 20m circle down to a 6m circle in the middle and then spiral out again, without bending his head too much to the inside.

▶ Try doing the exercises below on improving flexibility in the horse's poll.

'Thinking' for more roundness

To ask the horse to go on the bit, to round his back and soften to the bridle, instead of only working on the mechanics of riding him up to the bridle with your legs and seat, first picture what you want in your mind. Avoid thinking about just getting the horse's head into position; instead **think** of him being shaped like an arched bridge from tail to poll.

Imagine the horse's hind legs swinging forward deeply under his body, imagine the feeling of the horse's back coming up towards your seat, filling out under the saddle area, and imagine the topline of his neck extending forwards and arching softly into the bridle. Feel and see the energy coming from his back legs through underneath you and forwards towards his head. See how much your thoughts and pictures can alter the horse's way of going with minimal aids, even down to how he carries himself without resistance.

Improving flexibility in the poll and neck

Many so-called hard-mouthed horses are often not so much hard in the mouth as stiff in the neck – supple the neck and the mouth gets softer.

Many (but not all) horses are quite stiff in the neck and poll. This naturally makes it more difficult for them to be soft and give to the bridle – although I must say again that the head is only a small part of properly getting a horse on the bit. If the horse is too soft or learns to back off and go behind the bit, things can be more difficult than ever, so be careful with these exercises.

If the horse is soft and he is able to give his head to each side, then the neck muscles will be such that he finds it easier to give to the bridle in front. Pulling the head back and forth with the reins or sawing on them is not horsemanship and is not what we are going to do here.

From the ground

To soften the neck, firstly stand on the ground next to the horse and position yourself alongside the saddle. Gently take up the rein nearest to you and apply light pressure to invite the horse to bring his head around to you. Don't pull his head around, just set it up and wait, so that when he yields he will release the pressure from his mouth. When his head has been around towards you for about five seconds let his head go straight again. If, instead of yielding his head, he moves his body around, move quietly around with him so that you are always in the same place next to the saddle.

Let him rest and stroke him for a minute or so between each try. Now do the whole thing the other side. A couple of times each way is enough for any session. Over a period of days or weeks you will find the horse becomes more willing to give.

If you agree with using titbits (I don't normally), instead of the reins you could use a carrot (for example) to ask the horse to bring his head around to the side in the initial stages. This is nice for the horse and has less room for human error, but it doesn't teach the horse to yield to the pressure of the bit.

From the saddle

At halt, with very long reins, apply the left leg gently, then start slowly and gently drawing the left rein out and around to you so that the horse yields his head a little to the left. Wait for about five seconds and release the rein, then the leg. Repeat it all on the right. Do the same twice each way. Eventually, if

Be imaginative with horses.

you always apply the leg before the rein, the horse will bring his head around just to the leg being applied, then when both legs are applied together, hey presto, he will give at the poll and drop his head to a light rein contact.

Why does riding 'on the bit' seem so difficult sometimes?

We want it too badly. Like many things in riding and life, the harder you try, the harder it gets! Trying too hard to get a horse on the bit causes unwanted tension in the rider and the horse.

The horse is too stiff somewhere in his body. It takes a lot of regular suppling for horses to work easily in a good outline. Most riding school horses fit into this category of being stiff. Learning to feel where the horse is stiff is a big part of being able to achieve great results. (See Chapter 17, on school figures, to find out how to develop that feel in your body.)

We're not setting it up and 'waiting'. This is similar to 'wanting it too badly'. Two and a half thousand years ago, Xenophon said that doing things by force with horses didn't produce the same delightful results; horses are much the same now and so are we, so instead of forcing things to happen, set things up and **wait** for the horse to give the right response.

The rider is too stiff somewhere in his/her body. Most of us are pretty stiff from everyday living. If you are too stiff then your body isn't very receptive to what the horse's body is telling you. It also makes it harder to flow with the horse effectively enough, therefore limiting his ability to expand into an outline. (See Chapters 3-5, on body position, hands and legs.)

The horse is mentally tense. If the horse is mentally tense: (a) his body will be too tense to work properly; and (b) he won't be fully listening to your aids.

Scan through your body and the horse's body to feel for any areas that are blocking the flow of energy. Dissolve the blocks by breathing into them or consciously letting them go.

Rein contact too tight. If the reins are too tight on a horse whose back is 'upside down', i.e. it is concave as opposed to the convex shape we want, the rider stops the horse from being able to change the shape of his back. Sometimes lightening the contact a little actually assists in getting the horse on the bit.

Rein contact too loose. Sometimes in our desire to be light, soft riders, we don't offer the horse enough help with his balance and by having the reins too loose it may be that we allow too much energy to 'fall out the front', rather than containing and directing it into the desired outline.

Things to do...

1. Experiment with riding horses in varying amounts of collection, from long, low and loose to more shortened, rounded and into the bridle.

2. 'Feel' through your own body and the horse's body to detect any stiffness that might hinder being able to work on the bit more easily.

3. Check whether the horse is mentally calm before trying to really shorten him up.

4. Look carefully at pictures of horses in the 'Horses for Sale' section of magazines and see if you can see which horses are working properly through their bodies and which ones have just got their heads held in to look posh!

5. Read Chapter 17, on school figures.

Quick reference...

Horses don't HAVE to be on the bit to be ridden; it is a 'whole body thing', not just about head position; set it up and wait; visualise and think what you want; let it happen; give horses frequent rests from being on the bit; being on the bit is part of an on-going suppling process.

Chapter 19

Taking lessons

Your goals

What is it you are aiming for with your riding, and what do you want to learn? These are the first questions to ask yourself with regard to the type of lesson and teacher you need. For example, if all you really want to do is hack safely and quietly around the countryside, do you need to be grinding around doing high-school dressage every week? There are horses for courses, and there are teachers to suit all manner of requirements. They are not all the same.

What you learn is important, whatever your aims, because if you have not been taught the right things in the first place, you have to unlearn all that old stuff before you can take on board the new. It is far more difficult to unlearn than it is to learn the right things in the first place. Hopefully this chapter, and this whole book, will help you to figure out how to know whether you are on the right track or not.

Teacher checklist

Be inspired, then see if you can also inspire the horse. Just think where your combined inspiration might take you.

Here are some things you could ask yourself about the tuition you are receiving:

▶ Do you learn something positive each lesson?

▶ Do your teachers explain things to you?

▶ Are they patient?

▶ Is it fun?

▶ Do they tell you when you are doing something right?

▶ Do they control their temper?

▶ Do they waste lesson time talking about their personal life?

▶ Do they help to show you how to do things by riding the horse?

▶ Do they spend too much of your lesson riding the horse?

▶ Do the horses like them?

▶ Are they an inspiration to you?

▶ Do they care about your progress?

▶ Are they safety conscious or careless?

▶ Do they explain things in different ways, or keep shouting the same thing in the hope that you will 'get it?'

▶ Do the things they tell you 'feel' right to you and the horse?

▶ Do they adapt to each pupil's needs and ability?

▶ Are they positive and encouraging or do they make you feel small?

Keep an open mind

Whilst many people like to think they know it all, when it comes to horseman-ship, nobody has all the answers. Anyone who thinks they have the monopoly on the truth is best avoided, since they are no longer receptive to new ideas. Sooner or later a horse or a pupil will come along for which they need new ideas, and that is the point at which either the horse, the pupil or they them-selves will suffer.

Patient teachers

Expect the teacher to be as patient as you need them to be. Let's be honest, if you already knew what they were teaching you, you wouldn't need to pay them to teach you, and they'd be out of a job (probably sleeping on the streets and dreaming of a life working with horses!)

Everybody learns at a different rate. A good teacher is able to work at whatever speed each pupil can cope with.

It is a skilled teacher who finds even small things to say to compliment and

The teacher needs to be respectful of the pupil, and the pupil needs to be respectful of the teacher. Horses treated with respect make happy horses; the same goes for people.

encourage the pupil, but it is unfortunate that many teachers (often, it seems, among teachers who are truly gifted riders) are not able to do this. If a teacher is being unpleasant, remember that is their problems coming to the surface. If someone tries to give you a gift and you don't accept it, the gift still belongs to them. It's the same with unpleasantness. If you don't take it on board, it still belongs to the owner. Let them keep it! You don't want their problems; you just want their knowledge.

Always ask 'why?'

Good communication is vital for good teaching. When you teach, you communicate the appropriate information in a way that the pupil can understand. If you are the pupil and you don't understand, then in order to learn you need the teacher to explain the thing to you in a different way so that you do understand. If you don't 'get it', it doesn't mean you're stupid. It means the teacher isn't speaking your language, and there are as many views on language as there are people on the planet!

Since riding teachers can be intimidating and/or you don't want to appear dim-witted, you may feel reluctant to ask them why you should carry out a certain instruction when riding:

Repeating the same information in the same way over and over is as pointless as shouting 'Where are the toilets?' over and over and louder and louder to a non-English-speaking Frenchman. (If you want the toilet, you'd better find another way of asking, before there is an embarrassing accident!) Likewise your teacher's responsibility is to find other ways to help you to understand the lesson.

'Heels down' – WHY?

'Outside leg back to canter' – WHY?

'Ask for canter in the corner' –WHY?

'Shorten the reins' – WHY?

'Put him on the bit' –WHY?

'Half-halt' – WHY?

'Keep your legs on' – WHY?

'Sit up straight' – WHY?

If the teacher doesn't answer your questions adequately, ask the question again. If they cannot answer you satisfactorily, ask someone else and/or change teachers ... it's your money! There is every chance that the teacher who doesn't give satisfactory answers does not know, but is trying not to admit it.

Sometimes you are told to do things in lessons that just don't relate to how you feel, e.g. 'sit back more'. It is important to realise that sometimes our feelings are not accurate and the teacher may well be right. One of the greatest learning tools is the video camera. Use it regularly to film a few minutes of

> Discover something new about riding and horses **every** time you ride.

your riding or lessons and you can double your learning, since it connects what you feel to what you are actually doing. The video gives you perfect feedback about what you are doing and what you need to improve.

'Every time I change teachers they tell me something completely the opposite to the last one'

Everyone has their own slant on things. Finding a teacher who really 'rings true' can be quite difficult. A qualification doesn't mean that someone is gifted at teaching, seeing, correcting and communicating; it means they passed an exam. When I passed my driving test the examiner said, 'You've passed, Mr Wood, now you can go off and learn to drive properly.' (And I'm still trying!)

Armed with however much or however little knowledge you have, it is up to you to be discerning and decide who is the right teacher for you. **This is an important decision**. As you gather experiences you will be able to know what is right and what is wrong for you.

Read as many books on the subject of riding as possible. What I find interesting is that there is far less contradiction between equestrian books written by great masters over the centuries, even from diverse traditions, than there is between one riding teacher and another in the same riding school ... it really makes you wonder.

Things to do...

1. Make a list of all the things you would most like to ask your teacher. Then go ahead and ask them!

2. Read as many books on riding and horsemanship as you can lay your hands on. How does the information compare to what you are told in lessons?

3. Ask to be taught by the same person each week, rather than whoever happens to be free that day.

4. Even if it is only on one occasion, get some individual tuition from someone who you think would be far too good for your current level – even if they are the best in the world, it doesn't matter. How does your regular lesson compare with the teacher or rider who is 'out of your league?'

5. Remember: YOU ARE THE PAYING CUSTOMER, not just a 'squaddie' to be yelled at by the sergeant major in the middle of the arena. It's your money!

Quick reference...

There must be respect between pupil and teacher; ask questions; know what you want to learn; video your riding; read up on the subject; everyone has different ideas; you are the customer; nobody knows it all; you can always go to another school.

Chapter 20

Sideways movements

I t can be hard enough to get horses to go forwards and backwards really well, but it is also pretty important to be proficient at getting them to go sideways too. Some of the advantages to be gained from sideways movements are:

▶ Improves the rider's overall control of all four quarters of the horse.

▶ Makes the horse more responsive to the aids.

▶ Makes the rider able to use the aids more effectively.

▶ Improves the rider's feel of what the horse is doing.

▶ Improves the horse athletically; makes him more supple.

▶ Makes the horse more 'useful', e.g. opening and closing gates when riding out.

▶ Improves the horse's self-carriage.

▶ Looks good and impresses onlookers!

So, it sounds as though learning to do this will be pretty worthwhile then.

Many riding books give detailed descriptions of the individual sideways (lateral) movements, and there isn't space in this book to go into that detail, so here is just a brief list of them.

Gymnastically beneficial to the horse: shoulder-in, travers, renvers, turn on the hindquarters, and half-pass.

Not really gymnastically beneficial (but worth doing anyway): leg-yield, full pass (or full travers), turn on the forehand.

As luck **wouldn't** have it, the gymnastically beneficial movements are harder to do. (Damn!)

We won't concern ourselves here with the ins and outs of each of these movements, but instead look simply at the basic ideas behind getting horses to go sideways. Once you've got the feel of the basics you can go on to learn and refine all the individual lateral movements with relative ease.

Getting the feel of sideways

Leg-yield on the ground

Think of each individual sideways step as an event in itself.

The best way to get a clear idea of the feel of lateral work is to walk the movement yourself, on foot, without a horse.

Leg-yield is just as it sounds; the horse yields away from one of your legs so that he goes sideways and forwards at the same time.

To effectively ask the horse to go sideways you need a pretty clear idea in your mind what you want.

▶ Put your hands in a rein position (this is important) and walk around the outside track of the arena. (Don't worry if you look or feel like a complete idiot, riding horses is a fairly crazy notion in the first place!)

▶ When you get to letter A or C – that's the middle of the short side – turn down the centre line, looking straight down the school.

▶ Keep looking and facing your body and hands straight down the school to the opposite end, but walk a 45° line back to the track, so that you are going sideways and forwards at the same time. You will have to cross one leg over in front of the other to do this, just as the horse will.

▶ **Don't turn your body or head towards the direction you are going, keep them looking straight down the school, parallel to the track.**

Congratulations! You have just done a very nice leg-yield. When it gets really comfortable, try it on the horse.

Leg-yield on the horse

Practise first in a nice, slow walk.

> Horses are 'into pressure' creatures, so if you press with your leg to move the horse over, he will probably press back into your leg and not move over very well at all. Make the leg aids light and support with a stick instead.

▶ **As the horse comes off the track at letter A or C to begin his leg-yield, put your leg on him behind the girth so that he yields away from it and steps sideways.**

▶ When you put a leg on the horse it usually means go forwards, so you need to let him know that you don't just want him to go forwards faster, but to go sideways instead. You do this with a momentary half-halt on the rein that is on the opposite side to the leg you are using – that sounds weird, but trust me, it is correct.

▶ **Keep your hands on the correct sides of the horse's neck. Don't cross the hands over the wither or try to push the horse sideways with the reins: that is not leg-yielding, it's rein-yielding. It doesn't work so well, doesn't teach you anything, and doesn't look nearly so cool!**

▶ As you feel him slow slightly in response to the rein, give a touch of the leg, then the rein, then the leg, etc. For example, if he's going to move sideways towards the right, use right hand, left leg, right hand, left leg, right hand, left leg, and so on.

▶ **The leg aids need to last no longer than one step of the horse, and must be at the moment when his hind leg is starting its step (when you feel his belly going in the direction of the sideways step, that is the moment to give the leg aid).**

▶ The hand aid, too, must last no longer than the duration of one footfall.

▶ **Keep your head, eyes, hands and body facing forwards, toward the far end of the school. Don't face the direction in which you want the horse to travel or he'll not step sideways. Instead he'll turn himself and walk in a straight line to the outside track.**

▶ Have your weight fairly central.

▶ **The main thing is to set it up before the first stride, and then let it happen.**

▶ It is very hard to 'fix' lateral work once it goes wrong. If it does go 'pear-shaped', stop, come around and start again.

Don't spend too long doing lateral work in any one session. It can be a strain on the horse's joints and can fry your brains.

Preparation is the magic ingredient

The best preparations for sideways movements are to learn to turn and do circles with the horse's head almost straight and without using the inside rein more than the outside. (See Chapter 5, on hands, fist, elbow and wrist.)

It is also ideal to learn to be able to feel which of the horse's legs is moving at a given time (see Chapter 16, on the three paces), since doing sideways stuff means you will be directing a particular leg to go in a particular direction at a particular moment. (Wow!)

It is important to think about the principles and ideas of giving the aids (see Chapter 7, 'Is it a bird, is it a plane or is it an aid?'). It is no good giving a half-halt that doesn't work, and then carrying on as though it did. You need to be honest with yourself, and if it didn't work make the right decision, know that you need to ask again a little more firmly.

I'll admit that this all sounds pretty hard, but it's easy when you get the feel of it, and very satisfying too. When you first start driving a car it turns your head into spaghetti thinking about 'mirror, signal, indicate, clutch, change gear, oh damn missed second gear, clutch, gas, steer the corner, traffic lights, clutch, aarggh ...' but pretty soon you can drive with the radio pumping, tapping the steering wheel to the beat, and be chatting away to a passenger without too much difficulty at all (not that I'm advocating this as a sensible way to drive!). Lateral work is the same. It seems that there are so many things to think and feel to get it right at first, but once you get the feel, it's easy... kind of!

Pitfalls

The most common pitfalls are these:

1. Trying to make it happen by bending the horse's head too much.

2. Tipping your weight off to one side too much.

3. Not keeping the direction of your body and eyes in line with the horse's head.

4. Allowing the horse just to keep ploughing forwards through the bridle instead of going sideways.

5. Not timing the leg–hand–leg–hand sequence with the horse's legs.

6. Trying to fix it once it's gone wrong,

7. Trying too hard; forcing it to happen rather than setting it up and letting it happen.

8. Using the leg too strongly instead of a light leg and a tap with the schooling stick.

Things to do...

1. Watch good riders and horses doing lateral movements so that you start to understand them and really let the movements soak in to your mind.

2. Learn about the details of the different lateral movements.

3. Practise on the ground.

4. Look for one or two good quality steps, instead of expecting to be doing graceful, sweeping canter half-passes with invisible aids!

5. Be patient and avoid trying to make it happen.

Quick reference...

Sideways movements done correctly have great value for horse and rider; get a clear feel of what you want; set it up and let it happen; do all the right preparation; be pleased with a little done well; keep the aids to a minimum; be sure you are moving the horse over with your leg and not the reins.

Chapter 21

'The magic tool': inside leg to outside hand

You may well have heard the expressions 'inside leg to outside hand' or 'diagonal aids'. If you haven't before, you have now! This brilliant technique is one of the real foundation stones of quality riding. It may take a while for you to establish the 'feel' of this tool, but it's worth persevering. One of my old master teachers admitted it had taken him a considerable time to get the feel of it when he was learning, so be patient, keep it simple and 'feel' for it, as I have attempted to describe below.

What uses does it have?

Because it acts diagonally 'across' the horse, this little technique helps to balance or rebalance the horse; it is used if the horse is 'falling in' towards the centre of a circle; it can be used in exactly the same way if the horse is 'falling out' (believe it or not!); it is used for quality lateral work; it is used to straighten the horse; it is excellent for keeping the horse light on the reins; and it is a great element of bringing the horse on the bit in a harmonious way. Sounds like it is worth learning, hey?

What does it mean?

Essentially it means that you give a momentary aid (signal) with the inside leg, followed by a momentary half-halt aid with the opposite hand, i.e. the outside hand. OR you do it the other way round: the hand first, followed by the leg.

Ask yourself: 'Am I pressing the horse with my leg, or suggesting?' Avoid pressing, develop suggesting.

(Hmmm.) (Let's be clear here: the inside leg is the one nearest the middle of the school; and the outside hand is the hand nearest the fence or wall of the school.)

The reason we use the opposite hand aid after or before the leg, rather than just the leg aid alone, is to let the horse know that the leg aid doesn't just mean 'go forwards more', which is what the leg normally means to the horse.

Because the hand checks the forward movement of the horse slightly, the extra energy created by the leg aid has to go somewhere, so it is directed sideways, for example.

(If we used the hand on the same side as the leg, e.g. inside leg and inside hand, the horse may fold up on that side by having too much bend. This would then cause his energies to 'escape' out of the outside shoulder and his balance to be disturbed, the same as if you turn the wheel of a pushbike too much it helps you to fall off the opposite way! That all sounds very technical in words, but it makes sense to feel it.)

How firmly should the aids be given and for how long?

The firmness of the aids obviously depends on how sensitive the horse is and how much he is listening to you. As you use this technique you will find that the horse will become more sensitive, so that eventually you may only have to **think about deepening your leg**, and **think about closing the hand.**

The key to success here, as with any aids, is to start out lightly and then repeat the aid a little more firmly if the horse doesn't respond. Remember to be honest with yourself about whether the horse has responded and therefore whether the aid has worked. If not, repeat it. Sometimes it pays initially to use a schooling stick to gently encourage a response to your light leg aid.

It is important that the outside hand aid lasts only for a moment and is not so strong or lasts so long that the horse's head ends up facing to the outside!

In order for the leg aid to be really effective, it is very important that you feel a response from the horse to your light hand aid, which should be a 'feel' on the rein within the hand itself.

The timing is easy: the leg and hand aids should only last as long as it

Imagine you're a horse...

You are suspicious of anything new.

Using diagonal aids means you can affect the horse without him shooting forwards from both your legs, or bracing against both of your hands.

takes to say the words 'leg-hand', and should not be given simultaneously, but follow each other with the kind of timing of saying 'leg-hand' or 'hand-leg' in a relaxed way.

Keeping the circle and self-carriage

Many of us have struggled at some time or other to push the horse out onto the circle with the inside leg, but without the half-halt aid from the outside hand first, the leg is not effective: how can it be? We've trained the horses to think that leg means more energy, go forward or go faster! So instead of pushing and squeezing more with the inside leg to 'get the horse out', first do a momentary half-halt within the outside hand (not a pull or a jerk or sawing) and follow it by the leg. Remember the timing above. What you will find as you give these aids in the right way is that the horse will also improve his self-carriage and come more connectedly onto the bit for you. Wowee!

When you and the horse become really tuned in to this idea of inside leg to outside hand, you will even be able to do circles where the horse is bent nicely and looking to the inside, but he is only on the inside leg and outside hand, so that inside rein can actually hang loose! This gives the horse an irresistible space in which to place himself, so that he comes more and more on the bit with ever lighter aids and truly starts to carry himself.

What about hacking out or riding on a straight line?

Have you ever watched a dog running along from behind? Now I'm not suggesting you get arrested for taking an unhealthy interest in dogs' rear ends, but if you take a look you will see that they run crooked, with their hind end slightly out to one side or the other: horses are the same. So even when you think a horse is walking straight, there is always something going on, and often using diagonal aids as described above will help to straighten him.

Even if the horse is going pretty straight, you can use the diagonal aids to ask the horse to listen to you or to improve the horse's self-carriage, by imagining one leg being the inside leg and the opposite hand being the outside hand.

Sideways movements

Once you have the feel of this sequence of aids, lateral work is easy. In a very subtle way, each step of a lateral movement is the sequence of inside leg-outside hand, so a few steps of lateral work is made up of inside leg-outside hand-inside leg-outside hand-inside leg-outside hand-inside leg, etc.

It may sound complicated in words, but once you have the feel of it, this is a very natural pattern for the rider and for the horse, and a great tool to have in your horseman's kitbag.

Tips for success

- Hold your inside hand out a little so that the inside rein is two or three inches away from the horse's neck. If the inside rein is (incorrectly) held against the neck, you can be unintentionally moving the horse over with the rein, rather than with the leg. Holding the rein towards the inside of the circle away from the neck helps you not to trick yourself.

- Be honest about whether the hand or leg aid has worked, and repeat it if it hasn't, before giving the next diagonal aid. For example, if the hand aid hasn't worked, don't just give the next leg aid anyway.

- Look ahead and develop a feeling for 'inside leg to outside hand'.

- Make the aids as light as they need to be, but back them up as necessary if the horse doesn't respond.

- Be patient with yourself and the horse. This stuff isn't that easy. Be prepared for things to go wrong but stick to the principles and see if you can find the timing and feel for things to eventually go right. It is better for things to go wrong, but with you riding 'correctly', than for things to go 'sort of right' by using a concoction of incorrect techniques.

- Remember that the hand aid should only last as long as it takes to say 'hand', and the leg aid should only last as long as it takes to say 'leg'.

- Give the leg aid just as the inside hind leg is leaving the ground, i.e. when the horse's belly on the inside of the school is swinging towards the outside, or when you feel the saddle dipping downwards on the inside.

Chapter 22

Creative experimentation

t often pays to experiment with horses to see what results you get. It becomes possible to experiment with your riding and the horse once you are open to results and possibilities that you hadn't expected. Sometimes things come about with horses in ways you don't foresee.

Many of us are simply too afraid to experiment. We are raised to believe that there is a proper way to do everything and that that is **the** thing we must be trying to learn. Actually, every horse, every rider, every situation, every moment and every movement are different. This means that experimenting can be extremely useful.

In any experimenting you do, it must be your first consideration to be kind and loving to the horse at all times, and not do anything that risks your own or the horse's safety. However, that still leaves huge room to try experimenting in subtle ways, if you start to look for them.

Try:

► Relaxing a part of your own body to see if it alters the horse's way of going.

► Softening your jaw.

► Breathing more deeply.

► Relaxing your ankles.

► Having lighter stirrup pressure.

Create a partnership of equals: one where you and the horse are having an equally good time.

See what happens if you:

▶ Give a millimetre or two of the reins to the horse.

▶ Lighten your legs.

▶ Straighten his head a little.

▶ Ask for a smaller circle or a bigger circle.

▶ Ask for some transitions.

▶ Slightly bend the horse's head more to one side or the other.

▶ Slow the pace.

▶ Increase the pace, etc. etc.

▶ Use your imagination in all sorts of ways.

The combination of ways to experiment is infinite. The important thing is that with each little experiment you try, you then wait and watch receptively to see what response the horse gives you. Whatever it is, it is neither 'right' nor 'wrong', but it is useful for you to feel and observe, learn what happens when you do a certain thing with the horse, and log it in your mind as part of your horseman's tool-kit of knowledge.

Often experimenting will help you to hit on just the thing you need to get the end-result you want. Sometimes you will hit onto something even better than you hoped for, which means that, had you been limiting your riding, you would have limited the outcome and not been so successful! Wow!

Things to do...

1. Watch some successful competitors, and listen to what they say. Notice how the real winners are focused, and don't appear to be so desperate as the ones that just missed getting placed regularly.

2. Develop awareness and feel in your riding in every moment of every ride: THIS IS WHERE REAL RIDING BEGINS.

3. Experiment all the time to find out what works and what doesn't. Keep an open mind.

Quick reference...

Awareness is the key to developing feel; be in the present; experiment with yourself and the horse; focus on the 'means whereby', not the goal; lighten up and have fun! Use your imagination with horses.

Part 5

Horsemanship Work

It is uncanny how some people seem so good with horses and yet it can be hard to see what it is they do that makes a difference: that difference is horsemanship, and horsemanship **can** be learned.

In this section we will be looking at how to develop your horsemanship alongside your riding: a catalogue of good habits, at whatever level you are working.

Sound horsemanship not only makes you 'good' at handling horses in challenging situations, it helps you and the horse to understand each other, improves performance under saddle and enables you both to be safer.

Horsemanship is all about habitual common sense, keeping your eyes and your mind open and having the right attitude. Whenever you are handling or with horses, see the world through the horse's eyes, act with tact and intelligence, see situations as they arise (or even before if you can) and constantly update your knowledge, experience and your 'map' of how things are done around horses. Taking horses out into the world and being in varied situations with a variety of horses is the only way to expand your horsemanship: learn by experiences, preferably good ones!

Aspects of safety –
for the rider

'Ve been kicked, bitten, stamped on, knocked over, knocked about, bucked off, spun off, reared with, bolted with, dragged about, dragged down by self-doubt, daunted by challenges, looked over the abyss of my self-control, had fights I couldn't possibly win, backed down, bottled out, felt outwitted, been humbled, squashed into walls, suffered a sore back, sore legs, sore shoulders, a sore wallet, bashed my hip on tarmac, been high as a kite on adrenalin, so scared I've jumped off the horse and walked home, so apprehensive I've been in the bathroom for an hour before riding, had my hand mashed in a gate, had my feet flattened, been run over, been told 'that should teach you not to lean forward in canter' as I lay at the teacher's feet with a broken arm, held 500kg of prancing stallion while he covers mares, propped-up quivering mares while 500kg of testosterone-crazed stallion rears over us and takes the mare, I've been soaked to the skin and chilled half to death, sun-stroked, dripping with sweat, totally exhausted, completely lost in fog, told by my friends that I 'always smell of horses'... but I'm still doing it. Why?

Because it's GREAT!

Everyone who loves riding loves having fun around horses, but no one likes getting hurt. Horses are big, strong, fast and unpredictable; those are some of the things that make them fun and exciting, but they are also things that make them potentially dangerous. The only cast-iron guarantee of not getting hurt around horses is to avoid them altogether!

If you start thinking like a horse, you will see potential 'situations' before they happen.

Although being around horses brings with it an element of ever-present danger, there is a great deal we can do to lower the odds of getting hurt:

▶ Expect the unexpected!

▶ Develop a healthy respect for horse's strength, speed and survival responses.

▶ Acquire as much skill, self-control and competence as you can, on and off the horse.

▶ Develop a real understanding of what makes horses tick.

Awareness and 'habitual common sense'

Above all else, becoming aware of potential breaches of safety will help you to reduce or avoid harmful situations altogether. Anyone can develop this sense of awareness, both for themselves and for other people in the vicinity. This sense of awareness doesn't necessarily mean being really boring, never doing anything exciting with horses or getting neurotic. It just means engaging in 'habitual common sense'. You'd think that doesn't sound hard, but you see people acting without common sense around horses all over the world any day of the week! Mad.

Some ways horses can hurt you, and how to avoid it

They can step on your foot. When you are next to a horse, learn to notice when the horse's shoulder that is nearest to you is moving, because the shoulder has to move before the foot. See the shoulder moving as a little warning sign that your foot is about to be squashed. Experienced horse people tend to walk slightly pigeon-toed, without even thinking about it. That way their toes are less tempted to get underneath a horse's foot!

Short answer: don't leave your foot under the horse's!

They can bite you. Horses normally bite when they believe you are going to hurt them, or if you are causing them discomfort and you have not noticed their earlier, subtler, 'whispered' warnings! Avoid giving titbits, learn to tack up and groom in a way that is acceptable to the horse, avoid putting your hands out for them to bite. Approach the horse at the shoulder, not the head. If he

Remember: when horses greet each other and sniff noses, they can strike out with their front legs (and let out an offended squeal that makes you jump).

bites over the stable door, don't invade his space by trying to pet him. Respect his space by leaving him alone. Don't hit horses for biting – all it does is teaches them to bite quicker next time. Get expert help if you need to.

Short answer: don't be in reach of his teeth!

They can kick you. Many times when horses kick out, it is not at humans but at other horses, and the human is in the wrong place. Learn to notice where horses are positioned in relation to each other. Don't approach a horse's backside with any less politeness or warning than you would the backside of a human member of the opposite sex in public! That should save you some scrapes. Habitual kickers need expert handling, so if that's what you've got, get help.

Short answer: keep your eyes peeled, take nothing for granted and don't be there when his heels come flying out!

They can knock you over. Horses barge into each other, but they don't barge into the herd-leader very many times! Become his herd leader. Use your body language to look sure of yourself instead of looking like a pushover. Make a clear boundary in your mind as to how near you will allow the horse to be to you when you lead it, and stick to that boundary.

Develop an ability to see horses coming towards you out of the corner of your eye so that you can act in good time: a good horseman is like a good schoolteacher: they have eyes in their backsides.

Become really good at reading situations through the horse's eyes, so that you notice something that might make him run into you before it happens. Read the advice on leading in Chapter 25.

Learn to notice when you take little steps backwards away from the horse when it isn't necessary: every time you step back you are telling him he is the boss and inviting him to step on you at some time in the future.

Short answer: learn to be aware and effective on the ground; develop a real sense of body language, horse and human.

Imagine you're a horse...

You don't like small spaces, where you may not be able to run away from trouble.

You can fall off them. If you are going to ride, then at some point you are going to fall off – it's a simple as that. But you can increase or decrease the odds of it happening by various means, most of which are common sense, something that we often leave at home when we go riding! To a large degree it is possible to vary the likelihood of getting hurt by how well you develop a good, balanced seat. Time spent doing this is never wasted. Over-horsing yourself or over-facing the horse you are riding are great ways to create situations where you might fall off.

Short answer: Reduce the odds of falling off by learning to be good at staying on!

Keys to safety (through horsemanship)

1. **The ultimate, non-negotiable rule between myself and horses is this: I never let horses come into my 'space' uninvited. They must learn how close is acceptable – they weigh 500kgs, and that's a lot more than me, even after Christmas! There is no room for negotiation on this one.**

2. You wouldn't dream of driving a car with doubtful brakes or steering, yet it seems almost common practice to ride horses with neither! Don't even go there unless you really know what you are doing.

3. **A horse's hindquarters (i.e. the kicking equipment) normally turn in the opposite direction to his head, e.g. if the horse's head is turned to the right, his hindquarters will naturally go around to the left. Learn to see this as it happens.**

4. When you lead a horse, have his head bent slightly towards you. That way he is less likely to forget you are there. He is also less physically able to push into you with his shoulder.

5. **Look ahead when you ride. It improves your balance, helps you to stay on board and allows you to absorb the horse's movement more. (Most times when I've been bucked off I have looked down. Most times when I have sat to bucks I've remembered to look ahead.)**

6. Don't ride on roads unless you can control and move the horse's back end and front end sideways.

7. **Short, tight reins are a great way to pull yourself, or for the horse to pull you out of the saddle, over his shoulder and onto the deck!**

Horsemanship is a BIG subject.

8. Leading the horse on a short, tight lead rope pulls the horse into your space and pulls you into trouble.

9. **Horses can throw their heads up very violently. When you are around the horse on the ground, avoid having your face above his face, or you may be looking for a good cosmetic dentist!**

10. Don't over-horse yourself. That means not riding a horse you can't cope with, not riding in a situation you can't cope with or asking the horse for things one of you can't yet cope with. If you suspect you are over-horsed, the first course of action is to back-pedal immediately, take the horse home, get back to a place you can manage, dismount or swap with someone who can cope. Do whatever you can not to allow the situation to overtake you – there will be times when it will anyway, but don't stick at it simply for reasons of ambition, pride or to save face. Increase the challenges and difficulties with horses gradually. You can't improve your riding very much if you are in traction!

11. **Make sure horses know you are there. When they forget about your presence you are in increased danger of the horse acting more on instinct than training. When you are on the ground around the horse, make sure his eyes are on you, or whistle when you are out of sight (e.g. behind him) so that he knows it's a human behind him and not another horse (horses can't whistle!).**

12. Keep a distance from other horses under saddle. Horses naturally want to bunch up close, so I know this is not easy. Instead of trying to make your horse slow down to stay away from the horse in front, think of actually stopping your horse for a second or two. As soon as he checks his pace enough to make a space, carry on. Repeat this as necessary. It will help make a safer distance between moving horses.

13. **Leave the riding of 'dodgy' or 'problem' horses to experts. There are enough good horses in the world without riding horses with problems unnecessarily. Anyway, riding a 'problem' horse is more than likely causing the horse great distress too, and that isn't really fair.**

14. Better not to ride at all than to ride an unsuitable horse in unsuitable traffic conditions. This is a very serious point.

15. **In order not to make situations worse, develop the ability to appear nonchalant and non-reactive in the midst of crisis, whilst at the same time taking effective action. Now that sounds ridiculously hard: and it is!**

Things to do...

1. Enjoy yourself, but be sensible.

2. Wear the right kit.

3. Watch out for other people's safety around horses, as well as your own, e.g. don't turn your horse's back end towards someone else's horse.

4. Act with habitual common sense at all times.

5. Respect horses, without fear (if possible!).

6. Avoid being bitten, kicked, trodden on, knocked over; don't fall off or do anything that might hurt!

Quick reference...

Expect the unexpected; the only cast-iron guarantee of safety around horses is not to go near one; it's no fun being hurt; there are lots of things you can do to improve your chances of being safe; think about everything and be aware; watch out for other people and horses as well as yourself; traffic is serious; practise habitual commonsense; see every situation through the horse's eyes.

Chapter 24

The horse's safety

The thing that most horses think about more than anything else, apart from food, is their own safety! Practically all of their behaviour and reactions are a direct result of this preoccupation. If the horse feels safe, he will have more to give us in terms of attention, trust, willingness to learn and the ability to do good work.

How can we help the horse to feel safe with us?

▶ Develop a desire and intention that the horse should feel as safe as possible with us.

▶ Start looking at tiny clues in his behaviour to show us ways in which he may feel unsafe. Does he flinch when we do certain things around him? Does he have a worried look in his eye when we approach in a particular way? Does he not feel OK about hacking out in certain places with us? Does he show ways of 'self-protecting' himself when we ride, such as rushing, unwillingness to go forward, being 'jumpy' about the whip, gnashing his teeth when we pick up the reins, etc.? Is he afraid to be in a trailer etc.? The list of ways horses can show us that they don't feel safe is almost endless.

▶ Having recognised ways in which the horse may feel unsafe, it is our duty as

Imagine you're a horse...

Your memory is fantastic.

human(e) beings, to reassure the horse – in ways **that work for him**, not just in ways that we think would work for us – that he is safe. Telling him in English or patting him are not the most likely ways that the horse will find helpful. If we see him worried about a particular activity, maybe we can carry out that activity in a different way. Often just doing things more slowly is enough.

Here are some suggestions: If the horse is fearful of the whip, use it to caress the horse until he sees it as an instrument of delight. If the horse is afraid to be in a trailer it is essential to make the entire loading experience more pleasant –take as long as it takes and be as emotionally uncharged as possible. When loaded, the quality of the driving needs to be considerate enough to make the travelling experience as free from fear as possible. If the horse is afraid of the bit, maybe riding the horse on a lighter contact will work for a while, and maybe you can take time out to think about how you use your hands.

I was once loaned a beautiful six-year-old Lipizzaner mare (when someone loans you a horse as nice as that there's bound to be a catch!) that had been 'professionally' broken and schooled. The horse was so petrified of the bit that when anyone picked up just the buckle of the reins off her withers, she would violently throw her head in the air. This horse did not feel safe; this horse was not unique. My solution was to ride her in the school for weeks on end with the buckle resting on her wither and the whole rein hanging down. After three months or so, the horse had progressed to feeling entirely safe and I had worked around to her accepting the rider's hands and working beautifully on the bit. She finally felt safe.

It is important to remember that horses have great memories, and the things they remember more than anything are the experiences when they did not feel safe.

> Become more effective by being less and less predatory; know what your body language is saying in every situation.

Emotional control

One of our paramount duties in terms of the horse feeling safe is that the horse must be safe from our own unruly emotions **AT ALL TIMES**. Losing our temper, getting frustrated, getting over-ambitious, asking too much, fighting the horse, feeling anxious, and any manner of other negative emotions must always be kept away from the horse and never expressed or taken out on him. This is one the single most difficult things to learn to do around horses, but if you think about it, what possible right do we have to dump our negative emotions on the horse?

To be the finest horseman/woman you can be means being a consistent, calm and effective ally to the horse in all situations. If you lose control of your emotions around a horse, you have not only let the horse down, you have let yourself down too. Nobody is perfect, and we all slip up from time to time. If it happens, recognise it. Accept you have done it and resolve to do what you can to avoid it happening again. That way, you are truly on the path to becoming a finer horse-person, and a finer person-person too!

It seems to me that this idea of the horse feeling safe could be the subject of an entire book in itself (watch this space), but I hope that the above has at least outlined the idea and enabled you to begin looking at this incredibly interesting approach to being with these magnificent creatures.

Things to do...

1-6. Become aware of how the horse may feel unsafe and do what it takes to make him feel safe!

Chapter 25

Basics revisited: leading, tacking up and mounting

Leading, tacking up and mounting horses are things that we often do without thinking and don't necessarily put much value on, but actually, all three activities have contained within them many elements of communication, partnership and clues to how the horse will behave and feel when it is ridden. It is also a sobering thought that most horse-related injuries occur when they are being handled on the ground.

Reflections on leading

▶ Leading means to 'show the way', or to 'guide by example', not to drag or force (or to be dragged!).

▶ **Lead the horse in such a way that he feels as though he wants to follow you.**

▶ Leading the horse can be the beginning of a partnership and an art in itself.

▶ **Any moment when it feels possible, lead the horse as though the rope isn't there**.

▶ Think of the lead rope as a line of communication, rather than a means of control.

▶ **Imagine yourself being the horse – his instinct is to run from freedom, yet you have hold of him by the head.**

▶ See if you can lead the horse whilst walking in front of him, walking at his

When you're leading a horse, ask yourself what kind of 'leader' you would like to be for the horse.

shoulder and walking level with the girth.

▶ **If the horse is pulling ahead of you all the time, it tells you he may be impulsive to ride. Use the time when you lead him to show him to go at your speed. You can do this by stopping frequently and/or vibrating the rope until he moves back to the right place relative to you.**

▶ If the horse drags behind you all the time, it tells you he may be sluggish to ride, and may need you to ask for more energy from his hindquarters, perhaps with a light touch of a schooling stick.

▶ **If the horse is looking away from you, vibrate the rope to ask him to look towards you very slightly. That way he will remember you are there and be more attuned to you. He is less likely to barge you or step on your foot if his head is turned very slightly towards you.**

▶ If the horse feels soft through his head and neck when you lead him, he will probably be light to ride.

▶ **Make every effort to lead the horse without holding him under the chin, as that makes him feel restricted, claustrophobic and also pulls him into your space, making you less safe. Have some slack in the rope except for the moments when you need to correct him. As soon as the correction is finished let the rope go slack. This tells him he has done the right thing.**

▶ Make sure the rope isn't so long that the horse could kick you with his back legs.

▶ **Watch out for other horses that are in the area when you are leading. Remember that horses may 'have a go' at each other. Develop eyes in the back of your head and a sixth sense of what is going on around you.**

▶ If a horse really starts to pull or run away from you, make sure your body is immediately sideways on to him with both feet planted and still, rather than facing yourself forwards towards him. This stance, such as in a tug of war, gives you a more centred and powerful base.

▶ **If you are not wearing gloves and the horse really starts to 'turn up the heat', you are at risk of rope-burns, and need to make a decision whether to let go or not. Once it reaches this point you may not be able to hold him anyway, so you may as well save your skin, literally!**

▶ Pulling downwards on the rope is not a particularly effective means of control. Pulling slightly upwards and back towards the hindquarters is very powerful and should be used with great discretion.

Give the horse
'space' to be who
he really is – but
still have eyes in
your backside!

▶ **All the time you are leading the horse remember that your aim is to lead him quietly and obediently as though the rope were not there, so that there is always a feeling of connection between you without you needing to keep holding onto him. This depth of communication can be as satisfying as riding.**

▶ 'Be with' the horse when you lead him – two beings walking together.

Reflections on tacking up

Saddles

▶ Many horses are unhappy about being saddled. This is almost always the result of insensitive handling by a human or having to endure an ill-fitting saddle at some time in their life.

▶ It may help to let the horse have a good look and sniff of the saddle before you put it on.

▶ It is important that the saddle fits the horse well and doesn't dig in to him anywhere.

▶ It is important that the horse is not sore from the previous day's work before saddling him.

▶ Place the saddle on the horse very lightly and gently. This is not so easy with a heavy saddle such as a Western saddle, especially if the horse is 17.2hh and you are only 4ft10ins! If it is a real reach for you, stand on a box.

▶ Place the saddle a few inches further forwards than its correct position and allow it to find its own way back to the right place. Saddles will normally move backwards to the right place on the horse, but they rarely move forwards if placed too far back.

▶ To do up the girth, rest the **back** of your hand on the horse where the girth will go. Slide your hand under and across to get hold of the girth, but all the while keeping a contact with the horse with the back of your wrist or fore-

Imagine you're a horse . . .

You are physically very sensitive; you can even flick a fly off your skin.

arm. Draw the girth back over to your side of the horse, still keeping contact with the horse with your arm, wrist or back of your hand, and do up the girth **very quietly** and **loosely**.

▶ **Wait a moment or two and do the girth up again.**

▶ At this point it is worth maybe walking the horse around or doing a little in-hand work, before once more politely doing up the girth.

▶ **At no point in the procedure should you need to yank the girth up forcibly.**

▶ If the horse turns around to nip you as you do up the girth, it probably means he is afraid he is going to be hurt. Do not retaliate with your hand or shout. It will not help in the long run; it will just confirm his suspicions about you. Instead, as you do up the girth, leave the elbow which is nearest to the horse's head sticking out in the direction of his muzzle. Don't move the elbow or look the horse in the eye, just let him run himself into your elbow with his muzzle if he chooses to. You are not threatening him or warning him not to nip – if he chooses to do it, he runs himself onto your elbow. If you are not looking at him at the time, it is as though you aren't even there! **Be gentle with the girth!**

▶ The tightness of the girth is not like a seat belt in a car. It won't save you from falling off! The safest way not to tip off the side of a horse is to learn to ride with balance. How tight is the girth when you ride bareback? Precisely, there is no girth, just balance. You can learn to ride with balance as proficiently as anyone else does if you wish to work at it, and then the tightness of the girth won't be such a desperate measure.

Bits and bridles

Bits and bridles are another unnecessary area of contention between horses and riders.

It is easy for the horse or the rider to see the bridle and bit as a 'control' issue, or an instrument of torture. The way that you see the bridle is the way that the horse will see it. See it as a means of enhancing communication.

If you approach the horse holding the bridle as if it's some kind of fearsome gadget, the horse will believe you and not welcome the bit with an open mouth. If you handle the bridle and bit nonchalantly and with delicacy, the horse will soon learn to welcome it and open his mouth by himself.

Make sure the bridle and bit fit comfortably on the horse. Don't look for 'the right number' of creases in the corners of his mouth. Just like people, some

It is not the type of bit that matters, but the hands of the rider.

horses have thin lips and some have fleshy lips. What I do is put my fingers half way up the cheekpiece once the bridle is on and gently feel how much tension or slack there is in it. If it has a gentle 'give' in it, it is about right. Observe the way the horse works and reacts with the bit and bridle for any further adjustments. If the bridle is too tight then the constant pressure on the horse's mouth will make it numb and less sensitive and the horse therefore less pleasurable to ride.

Many people rush the bit into the horse's mouth because they appear to be able to create only a very short window of opportunity in which to shove it in before the horse's teeth clamp shut again. This is not ideal, since it makes the whole process seem unpleasant and forced, and usually involves the horse getting a bang on the teeth with the metal bit.

To make things easier, ask the horse to bring his head around towards you with your spare hand (assuming you have got three hands, that is!). This flexes his neck, makes him softer to handle and makes it harder for him to evade or react by throwing his head up and hitting his own teeth on the bit.

Put a finger well into the corner of the horse's mouth through the gap in his teeth, and tickle his tongue if you need to. Once he has opened his mouth to this, try to keep a finger touching his tongue through the corner of his mouth. While-ever you continue to do that he will be more inclined to keep his mouth open, giving you all the time in the world to put the bit in slowly, and proving to him what a cool customer you are when it comes to handling horses.

Many people forget themselves at the end of a ride and just pull the bridle off the horse. This bangs him in the teeth, And guess what? It makes him less inclined to have the bridle on next time!

To take off the bridle, slide it off both ears and hold the top of the headpiece, waiting for the horse to slip it out of his mouth. If he doesn't let go of the bit, put your spare hand in the corner of his mouth and look for his tongue to tickle again.

A short word about bits

For schooling purposes I usually use a plain old jointed snaffle. Sometimes I use a double bridle for more advanced horses. I start all my young horses with a rope halter, cavesson or bosal, riding them like this until walk, trot and canter are well established, before gradually moving over to using a bit. I find this gives me good communication and control of the young horse whilst preserving the mouth for more refinement.

As far as hacking out is concerned, I do not stick to a particular arrangement for all horses for all situations, I experiment, because every horse is different and every situation is different. In the schoolwork I consistently use the snaffle because it has a joint, meaning the horse can be worked more easily in different ways and separately on the two sides of his body. Also, with a snaffle there is usually less likelihood of evasions from the work than with other bits.

Reflections on mounting

Wherever possible use a mounting block. This saves your body, the horse's body, and the saddle and stirrup leathers.

I always mount horses when they are standing still. There is great value in taking the time to teach the horse to stand still for mounting, which carries over into riding. If he moves off without you asking, he is actually bolting with you, albeit very slowly. He may also be giving you less than his full attention and respect.

Sometimes horses move off a step or two when being mounted to adjust their legs or get their balance under the rider's weight. You can look at the horse's legs before attempting to mount and move him back or forwards until his legs look well-placed enough to take your weight, or you can gently rock the horse's shoulders from side to side to help him find the best balance to receive you.

If a horse consistently moves off as you are mounting, it may be worth staying exactly where you are and getting him to circle around you until he ends up back where he started. If he continues to move let him do so, but always on the same small circle around you, and always giving him the chance to stop in front of you where you wish to mount. With your patience the horse will learn what is required of him. This is how I back young horses: they learn to stand still, concentrate on me and adjust to my weight before we go anywhere.

If a horse stands still to be mounted by his own free will, i.e. with a little slack in the reins, he is saying he accepts you on his back. Conversely, if the horse needs to be coerced into carrying you, it is a good idea to ask yourself if he is really ready to be ridden or not.

If the horse is attuned to you during mounting, he is more likely to stay attuned to you when you are riding along. If the horse has his attention elsewhere as you go to mount him, firstly get his attention on you, vibrate the rein, or ask him to take a step back, or walk him around in a circle.

Mounting from the left is a throw-back to the cavalry, when the sword would be worn on the left hip, so mounting from the right would have meant the rider doing himself a real mischief with his own sword in a very nasty place!

Remember that when you mount a horse you are a predator climbing on the back of a prey animal!

Since we no longer wear swords, it is a good idea to become accustomed to mounting equally from both sides. At first this feels totally alien, but a little practice soon pays dividends. Try mounting from the right forty-nine consecutive times (with a mounting block at first) and it will feel as comfy as from the left.

One of my horses comes to the mounting block of her own free will at liberty (completely loose) to be mounted. The interesting thing is that, given the choice of which side I mount her, she chops and changes from day to day, depending how she feels. Just as she approaches the mounting block, she pauses and appears to make a conscious decision about which way she prefers to be mounted that day. What side would your horse favour?

Breathe out deeply as you mount and swing your leg up and over: it releases any tension in the process.

When mounting from the left, hold the mane or pommel and the reins in your left hand. Place the right hand over the top of the saddle to reach the opposite saddle flap, top of the stirrup leather or pommel. **DON'T HOLD THE CANTLE WITH THE RIGHT HAND**. Holding the cantle increases the chances of the saddle slipping as you mount, twists the saddle on the horse's back and makes you more vulnerable should the horse move off as you are mounting. There is a moment as you swing your leg over the horse when your right arm holding the cantle is in the way, and you have to let go with that hand. Try it and you will see what I mean.

Try to look ahead as you mount, it gives you a 'forward' perspective and means that if the horse moves off, you will have a better chance of moving with the horse rather than being left behind.

Bring your leg over the horse gently and slowly, lowering your seat into the saddle as though you are about to sit down on raw eggs and you don't want to make a mess on those nice clean jods. Horses' backs are more sensitive than most people realise, especially before the muscles are warmed up.

Before mounting, it sometimes pays to help the horse by doing a little in-hand work, lungeing or just walking around with the saddle on.

When mounting from the ground, do three or four little hops to get your springs going, and as you spring up, think of sending your head straight up over the other side of the horse's opposite shoulder. If you just think of going upwards, your body will feel as though you are falling back away from the horse, and your mind will not help you to spring up, because it unconsciously feels daunted by the idea of going straight up against the pull of gravity.

Teach or show the horse that he is required to stand still after mounting until you ask him to move off – you may want to adjust something (or send a text message) before you ride.

Things to do...

1-6. Think about how you habitually lead, tack up and mount horses. Practise all of the above and enjoy some real improvements in your relationship and results with these seemingly small details!

Quick reference...

The way a horse leads tells you about him mentally and physically; the ultimate aim is to lead as though the rope is not there; developing your leading and mounting skills are essential parts of fine horsemanship; the way we approach tacking up is essential; courtesy and fine observation are always required; make a friend of the horse, not an enemy; if it was important for Xenophon 2000 years ago, it's important for us now; mount from both sides; mount with consideration and physical self-control; mount a stationary horse!

Chapter 26

Crisis management

The more insight we develop into the horse's nature – e.g. what startles him, what upsets him, what the warning signs are, what he's thinking, etc. – the more chance we have of coping with any crisis situations. Time, experience and an ability to see the world through the horse's eyes are the keys to being most effective.

When we come upon any challenging situation for the horse, or anything that the horse finds new or suspicious, it is essential that we appear to be a trustworthy herd-leader and reassure the horse by our own confidence that everything is OK (sometimes easier said than done!). Maintaining an air of nonchalance, or even appearing to ignore the object and the horse's reaction to it, is often the best course of action. To do this means containing our own fears – not getting tense, breathing faster or holding our breath, gripping with our legs, yelling, letting our eyeballs hang out on stalks, tensing our two 'lower' cheeks, or, worst of all, grabbing with both reins.

Getting tense and losing control of your breathing and your eyeballs is like **agreeing** with the horse that things are not safe.

Gripping with your legs and grabbing both reins is **proving** to the horse that it's scary: 'Ok , Trigger, I've jumped on your back, grabbed your muzzle and got you by the "short and curlies" ... I'm the predator your mother always warned you about!'

Being jumped-upon and having his head or muzzle grabbed is how the horse would be attacked by a predator. His natural reaction is to think that he is being set upon and he will instinctively panic and want to run.

In an effort to appear more nonchalant in the face of difficulties, I some-

> Ask yourself: 'Am I letting my emotions overtake me?' Become an oasis of calm for the horse to come to, by being as emotionally uninvolved as possible.

times find that whistling something totally inappropriate like 'Agadoo' or 'Onward Christian Soldiers' does the trick. Something else that helps, if you can do it, is actually to laugh about the situation while it is happening. Horses seem to find it difficult to be scared when you're laughing.

Reading the signs

> When you grow past the need for 'control', you will truly start to experience the dizzy heights of possibility with horses.

The best way to deal with crisis situations is to read the signs and take avoiding action, ideally **before** anything goes pear-shaped. So what are the signs?

RHYTHM: If the rhythm becomes less regular, you know something's amiss. Make a mental note of it.

EARS: Where the horse's ears are pointing is where his mind is. Make a mental note of it.

HEAD: The head position is a huge indicator. If it's not straight (without you holding it straight with the bridle) or if it's stuck up in the air, the horse is distracted and contemplating flight-mode. Make a mental note of it.

BACK: If the horse's back is feeling tight and tense, then so is his mind. Make a note of it.

OTHER HORSES: When you are riding in company, if the front or back horse becomes more edgy, your horse will **definitely** notice. Notice it yourself.

HERD-REACTION: If another horse in the group takes off unexpectedly, your horse will almost certainly react. Catch him before he's finished taking even his first stride. Stay upright in your body, keep looking ahead rather than down at the horse, keep both legs in gentle contact with him, and bring him onto a small circle if you need to. The circle can be as small as three metres in diameter. **Don't just pull both reins as hard as you can and hope for the best – the best won't happen that way**!

THE OUTSIDE WORLD: Look at the world through the horse's eyes. Learn to see what things scare horses and make a note of them so that you are always prepared. If you detect a sheep behind a hedge, notice it before the horse does. If there's a pigeon's nest he's afraid of at the top end of the school, don't go there

Imagine you're a horse...

You have the instinct and ability to run like hell out of trouble.

in a confrontational way. Wait until he's well worked-in and gradually end up there by riding a string of circles that move up the school. If it is 'dustbin-man-day', remember in the back of your mind that Mrs Wigglebottom at number 23 always leaves her refuse rubbish bags lurking in the gateway like a coiled horse-eating monster, etc.

Energy levels

> If there's too much energy in the horse, lower your own energy levels and soak up some of his. Breathe out a lot!

Horses have a huge capacity for work and most stabled horses get nowhere near enough exercise. Wild horses do around twenty miles every day. And they are not even corn-fed or pampered. The more high-energy feed and the less exercise the horse has, the more his instinct to shy and run will surface. Take account of how high on energy the horse is before asking anything unwise or going into scary or risky territory.

Sometimes it helps to take off some excess energy with circle work, thoughtful lungeing or something similar before getting into a fight or riding out in open spaces. I spend a lot of time with my horses, so I can usually judge their energy levels by the look in their eye, the way they lead out of the stable and stand to be mounted. If they fidget at the mounting block they are probably brimming over with feel-good factor.

Crisis management (yikes!)

Whoever you are, sometime or other a horse will share a crisis situation with you. The difference between an expert and a novice is how you deal with it. Experts normally react so fast that there is only a very small crisis to fix – the horse may only manage to run a few yards, if that! The sooner you catch the horse from running, the easier it is to deal with.

Tricks for handling horses on the ground

Effective communication with a horse on the ground is a good foundation for riding. Getting his attention and lightness on the lead rope can be rewarding and make things a lot safer.

Notice when a horse you lead is not paying attention to you or not mentally 'with you' and do something about it before there is a battle of strength involved.

If the horse is pulling you, you are most likely giving him something to pull against. Use an intermittent contact on the rope by vibrating, wiggling, shak-

> Be adaptable and able to change; be fully responsive and responsible **in the moment.**

ing, or jerking it if you really have to (sometimes you may need to be firm, but that doesn't require you to be mean or crude), so that he won't have something steady to use his strength to pull against.

If the horse starts pulling ahead of you or strongly around to look, gawp or stare at something more interesting (and remember **NOTHING** is ever more interesting than what you're doing) start to wiggle the rope **lightly**, two to four times per second, and more and firmer if you need to, increasing the intensity of the movement order to match the seriousness of the situation, until his head comes around to you, then **IMMEDIATELY** he responds you must stop wiggling, smile and go back to 'neutral'.

Be willing to do the above correction as many times as necessary, possibly a few million. I'll bet he gets bored and stops pulling first, way before a million.

The most important part is this: the split second he responds, ideally to the lightest wiggle of the rope, don't get firmer, STOP wiggling, put slack in the rope and go neutral.

Always aim to lead horses on a loose rope. (The various methods and benefits of effective leading have already been discussed in the last chapter.)

Tricks when riding the horse

How do we deal with the unwanted use of strength in a riding horse? Obvious: get a **really** savage bit in his mouth, and show him who's boss ... (only kidding!).

Purists say, 'If the horse is properly schooled it shouldn't pull.' Absolutely right, but it's not always that simple, and anyway, who is going to do all this 'proper schooling' of every riding horse on the planet? Now let's get real.

Use horse sense and forethought wherever possible to avoid putting yourself and the horse into situations where he will get over-excited, too headstrong, unbalanced or scared into pulling.

Sometimes forethought doesn't help, so let's look at the structure of the horse's neck and buttocks. (Urgh?)

Horses have two parallel sets of muscles running up either side of the neck. If they tense both sets of muscles at the same time, they can employ their maximum neck strength. When we pull both reins together at the same time, we help the horse to use his maximum pulling power. If we bend the horse's neck to one side (as little or as much as we need to), the muscles on that side of the neck relax. As if by magic the horse is only half as strong in the neck as he was.

I heard a wonderful story about the late great Nuno Oliviera, who sat quietly on a horse and smoked a whole packet of cigarettes whilst waiting for the horse to cross a puddle – an expensive puddle, I'll admit. But the horse eventually crossed calmly and without the need for force. My bet is that the horse would not be afraid to cross a puddle the next time, because his memory of the event would be a calm one.

Actually, when horses are strong to ride it isn't that they are 'strong in the mouth' so much as strong in the neck, that is why working on suppling the neck can be of great value.

Apply the same principle, if necessary, to halve the strength in the horse's back end. If we shift the horse's rear around to one side or the other, e.g. in a small circle, it is more difficult for him to use his back end power against us, and easier for us to direct his strength into our service.

> Strong riders sometimes use their sheer physical strength and power, the bridle, a whip, a strong, active seat or spurs to overcome the horse's instincts. This doesn't always work in the long run, and often makes things worse by proving to the horse that it was a scary situation after all. This approach, rather than tact and patience, does little to build a partnership with the horse.

Rubbish bags and fighter aircraft!

People are often surprised by a horse's fear of something harmless like a black bin liner and yet they are able to ignore things that we perceive as potentially more dangerous, like fighter aircraft. The explanation for this is simple. Horses fear anything that might represent their natural predators, so anything about the size of a big cat (black-bin-liner-panther, for example) that is lurking in the hedge or near to the ground, ready to pounce, is what disturbs them the most. Once you start to look at the world through the eyes of a creature that gets eaten by big cats or wolves lying in ambush, you develop an ability to understand the horse's behaviour more and to take more appropriate action, often before anything starts to go awry.

Things to do...

1. Try to appear relaxed and nonchalant in the midst of chaos, whilst, of course, being effective. If the rider starts panicking too, the horse may really 'lose it'. If the rider gives an impression of being casual, the horse will often follow that example – easy to say, I know! Even if you're sitting on the horse wishing you'd worn your brown jodhpurs that day, try to not let the horse know it!

2. Looking ahead and not looking down is important. Sometimes a horse is hard to stop, but if the rider looks ahead he may be able to guide the horse to take a safer route. Looking ahead will also help the rider to 'sit', maintain more secure balance and stay on board over certain objects the horse may jump.

3. Sit up. Remember horses can stop as fast as they can go, so don't tip forwards too far, or you might not stop when he does!

4. Making soothing noises under your breath can help to ease tensions, both in the horse and the rider. By quietly saying 'Steeaaaady, steeaaaady' or some other soothing and optimistic phrases to him, you'll influence yourself to give better signals, and let him know you're there. Shouting is not a very wise option!

5. Often, in the heat of the moment, horses forget you're there, then suddenly see you on their backs, and it scares them to death. I've been bucked off a regular riding horse because he forgot I was there when my coat flapped out in the wind. As he saw my coat his instinct kicked in with 'Cripes, let me get that funny-looking demon off my back.' He was so panicked he bolted all the way home, jumped right over a cattle grid and couldn't be caught for an hour. Talking quietly or just lightly vibrating one rein can help avert difficulties by reminding the horse you are with him.

6. Rehearse in your mind the drill of being able to gather up the reins from the buckle to a contact in a split second.

7. Rehearse in your mind the drill of automatically bringing horses round on a small circle in a split second. Sometimes a horse has so much desire to move that holding him on the same spot with both reins can cause a rear or make things worse. That's where going in a small circle can help, so that he feels as though his energy and his feet are going somewhere, even if he's not! The small circle stops him from getting up a real head of steam.

Quick reference...

Learn what scares horses; read the signs before things go wrong; train yourself to turn horses automatically; keep the horse's attention on you; look ahead, not down; sit up; avoid getting into situations you or the horse can't handle; stay cool and appear to be a confident leader.

Chapter 27

Freedom, fun and fresh air

This is what it's all about: all the schooling, learning, training, dressage or whatever you want to call it, is all preparation for putting your riding to use. There is no better way to have fun, thrills, spills (occasionally) and see the countryside than on a horse.

Being outside, sharing the experience with a good horse, going at the speed you want to go, taking on little challenges along the way, being in good company or alone, enjoying the view from a different perspective, having a few more close scrapes and exciting moments than you get from the car window or walking on your own two feet, can be heaven on earth. Things may not always go to plan, it's true, but that's another story!

Cantering or galloping on a horse in the outdoors gives you the chance to experience the horse's life-force, joy, speed, sense of freedom and natural ability, as though you have borrowed his wings for a time. It's a real buzz, but there are even more benefits to riding out than just good old-fashioned bags of fun.

Benefits

Riding out gives you the chance to put things into practice, avoids you getting overly focused on schooling details, gives the horse a sense of variety and fun (horses love having fun), is a good way to get the 'freshness' out of a horse and teaches him to be more worldly.

As well as improving the horse's mind and attitude, riding out also helps to

Horses are naturally inquisitive creatures; they find it stimulating to have variety in their lives by going to different places with us and sharing pleasant experiences.

build up the horse's body in the right way, especially if there is hill-work involved. Going over different terrain teaches the horse to look after himself, watch where he puts his feet, improve his balance and ability to stay upright – all of which are rather desirable attributes if you want to ride him!

Going up hills strengthens the horse's hindquarters, whilst going downhill teaches him to get his hocks underneath him and become more supple in the joints of his hind legs.

My first horse was a ten-year-old ex-show Arabian who had lived her entire life on an immaculate Arab stud where the fields were so flat you could play billiards on them. When I started riding her outside she used to fall all over the place, tripping up on every tuft of grass and flopping down every slope. It took about two years of constant hacking for her to get wise about uneven ground.

Riding outside also has tremendous benefits for the rider. It improves the seat and balance, especially going up and down hill, in a way that school riding never can. It helps the rider to understand the nature of horses in more depth and to see how they react to various situations. It sharpens the rider's reactions and puts hours in the saddle 'on the clock'; if enough outside riding is done it helps to relax the rider and teaches them to become more natural and 'at one' with horses. It also gives the rider a great sense of achievement, especially once they've got back from a good exciting ride in one piece and are sitting in the hot tub or the pub!

Partnership

There is something about hacking that gives both you and the horse a sense of partnership. Horses are naturally nosey; they wouldn't normally have the courage or motivation to go as far or to the places that we take them out riding, so they get to experience and see new things. Horses would never get round to booking themselves into shows or the like, but going along with us means they can really enjoy a good day out being nosey. It keeps life interesting. As a young child, how much more fun was it to go on a school geography trip for the day than sitting in class? All these shared experiences are fun for the horse and can help to build a sense of partnership.

Horses are real 'tourists'. They just love going around saying, 'Ooh, look at that', or 'Ooh, that's an interesting-looking garden', or 'Oh, I've never noticed those ponies in that field before! To make a horse into an all-round useful and worldly 'being', it is important to give the horse (and yourself as a rider) as many of these positive experiences as possible.

Having a horse rather than a mountain bike has another advantage aside from sharing the hacking experience with a companion: horses normally look where they're putting their feet, freeing you up to enjoy the vista.

Schooling 'on the trail'

Whilst it is good practice to let the horse have more 'slack' and be more chilled out about the way he is going when you are riding out together, there are also lots of opportunities for doing the odd bit of schooling outside. This is a great way to keep things fresh and interesting, and anyway, all the things that you have done in the school will most likely need to be covered again outside, because horses are generally in a different mental state and 'space' outside, usually more forward and impulsive and not quite so responsive or listening to the aids. It is important to bear this in mind when outside and not expect or ask for as much to begin with as you would in the school. Here are a few ideas:

▶ As you walk happily along a lane, try some leg-yielding or half-pass across from one side to the other.

▶ When you come to gates, think about moving a specific part of the horse in a particular way – turn on the forehand, then rein back, then another turn on the forehand to get close enough to latch the gate. Then a few moments in halt, and then turn on the hindquarters to leave the gate.

▶ Try walk, trot, halt and rein-back transitions along a lane.

▶ Try doing circles around a bush or tree.

▶ You could maybe start to teach piaffe at a place where the horse wants to really go.

There are all sorts of ways to use the great outdoors to school yourself or horses, and it keeps the whole thing more interesting, especially for the horses. I've even cantered along in the sea near the shore and, as the horse hopped over the little breakers, asked for flying changes – beats surfing, any day.

Imagine you're a horse...

You have an active mind and a wide range of feelings and emotions.

Taking precautions

Riding out requires common sense. Here are some things to think about to make the outdoor experience a more positive one.

Although they generally enjoy riding out, many horses will soon become nappy unless the rider is mindful. It is perfectly natural and understandable for horses to be nappy, especially being ridden out alone, as the whole concept is against their nature as a herd animal.

To avoid things going down the slippery slope towards napping:

▶ Always try to ride a circular route, instead of turning round and going back the way you just came.

▶ Pick quicker paces on the way out from home – trot or canter a bit more – and just walk on the way home.

▶ If the horse starts jogging or getting excited on the way home, if there is a safe place, turn away from home again (ideally on a nice relaxed open rein – see Chapter 9 on effective steering), then turn back towards home, then away again, etc. in circles or figures-of-eight until the horse realises that you're not just going straight home. Stay calm and be prepared to ride away-from and towards home all day and all night, and all the next day if you have to. Hopefully someone will wonder where you are and bring you out some sandwiches and a flask of tea! Your patience will help you succeed.

▶ Try to pick different routes.

▶ Sometimes go for long, long hacks, in walk and a little trot., Most horses should be able to go all day like this. They have a huge capacity for this kind of work. I read an excellent piece in a Western training book about a difficult horse. The owners rode it thirty-five miles in one day to another town, mostly in walk, and then trailered it back home that night. The next day they did a similar thing. The following day a similar thing. The horse turned out to be perfect from then on. It just needed more work – as do many, many horses, but not the kind of work that can be given in a school situation. That horse also realised that every ride thereafter could end up being just as long, so there was no point wasting its energy messing about.

To school horses outside doesn't necessarily mean you have to go far. Sometimes I will take a horse just 500 metres from my front gate and do some training there instead of in the school. It still helps to give a different perspective.

> A horse who feels exactly the same on the way home as he did on the way out is quite rare.

> If a horse speeds up on the way home you can always turn around and go back out again immediately. You'll hear him think, 'Oh no, I've been sussed.'

Company

It is important to be polite to other riders when in company, and a good idea to pick polite and considerate riders to ride with you. Galloping past other riders with no warning, for example, is thoughtless, selfish, not fair on the horses and potentially dangerous for the other riders.

Weather and mental state

On wild, windy or excitable days, be aware that the horse may be over-excited and not so attentive to you. Pick paces and routes that will suit the conditions. Likewise, if the horse is 'off his head' and overly fresh due to lack of exercise or too much food, be sensible about what to ask of the horse, otherwise you just end up having a fight instead of a ride, and that is at least as unpleasant for the horse as it is for you.

Walking

Provided you and the horse are pretty good at leading safely, if things start going badly wrong, you may consider getting off and walking. It may give you more control. Also the horse may calm down because he can see you easily and doesn't think he's alone anymore, and he may be less 'wound up' by not having the aids applied when he is not in a fit state to respond to them. (Many accidents involving horses happen when the person is on the ground, so do consider how well you and the horse lead before doing this and make sure he stays out of your space at all times.)

Traffic

This is a whole subject in itself and there is not adequate room for it here. There is no question that, whilst horses can be dangerous, where horses and traffic meet things can get seriously dangerous. Be as sensible as you can be. If at all possible, avoid riding near traffic. Again, I know it's easier said than done.

Things to do...

1. Do loads of riding out in different places.

2. Slot in some little bits of schooling outside.

3. Get a feel of what is sensible to ask the horse on each particular occasion.

4. Enjoy!

5. Be sensible and safe.

Quick reference...

Have fun; riding out puts the theory into practice; it's great for the horse and the rider, physically and mentally; do it, do it, do it; it keeps schooling fresh; it helps develop a feeling of partnership; always consider necessary precautions; enjoy yourself.

Useful information

Perry Wood teaches **Real Riding** at clinics in various locations, trains horses and riders at all levels, and coaches corporate executives in their leadership through intra- and inter-personal skills using horses to effect high-speed change.

For more information about Perry Wood's **Real Riding** courses, workshops and clinics, visit his website: **www.realriding.net**

Glossary

Harmony: being in agreement with each other.

Horse sense: normal common sense, but used around horses. Horse sense is essential to use at all times where horses are concerned: excepting the fact that going near horses at all could be considered to be the opposite of common sense!

Repetition: doing or saying something over and over again: this is something that is indispensable for training horses and riders. Repetition also comes up quite a lot in this book, to help the reader connect the different aspects of horsemanship together, as well as it being helpful for us humans to hear the same thing more than once!

Confused: not knowing what is right or what to do – e.g. one riding teacher tells you one thing and another teacher tells you something else.

Poll: part of the horse on top of his head just behind the ears.

Habitual common sense: not being daft on a regular basis!

Teacher: someone you pay to help you to improve, not someone you pay to insult you.

Lesson: what you have in order to learn and to improve, not just a half-hour of physical exercise on horseback.

Consistent: always being the same, being reliable and always responding in the same polite manner. Consistent contact means that the contact has a steady and reliable quality: not limp then jerky, then hard, then wobbly, then oops! banged in the teeth, then like wet lettuce, then like a grip from Robo-Cop, then vague.

!: This is an exclamation mark. I use it a lot throughout this book, possibly too much, but if horses could write, I think they'd use this a lot too, especially when they watch our efforts at trying to get along with them sometimes!!!

Passive resistance: resisting without being active. (The dictionary says 'resistance to a government or law without violence, as by fasting or demonstrating'! So there you go – maybe try resisting the horse by missing out a couple of meals!)

Active: 'doing stuff', moving, working, pulling, kicking, being busy or getting involved.

Impulsion: forward urge that is requested by the rider: as opposed to forward urge that is the horse's idea!

Dumb: something horses are not.

Sensitive: something horses are!

Fear: the feeling of distress, apprehension or alarm caused by the thought of possible danger or pain. The equestrian extreme of this is the need to wear brown jodhpurs!

Courage: the commendable quality of doing something despite your fear, e.g. 'I need to wear my brown jodhpurs even to think about doing this, but I'm going to do it anyway.'

Acting: pretending to be someone else, or pretending to feel a certain way, e.g. acting cool, acting confident, acting like you know what you're doing, acting big, acting the fool.

Decisive: deciding what the right thing is; around horses it sometimes means judging things moment by moment; being sure what you want and expressing it clearly.

Tempo: speed or beats per minute, e.g. a ballad has a slower tempo than a techno dance-track or a thrash heavy-metal song.

Feel: this is a very indefinable quality to develop as a rider, a kind of subtle receptiveness, a sense of what to do when and how, of being able to be in the horse's shoes.

Pear-shaped: things not going to plan.

Balance: being at one with gravity, e.g. staying on the horse by balance rather than gripping with the legs or relying on the hands.

Horse-mode: thinking and acting in a more horse-like way.

Self-control: not losing it mentally, emotionally or physically!

Patience: something you need bags of to be good with horses!

Confidence: being sure of yourself.

Contact: communication, e.g. through the reins.

Expected: when something you thought would happen actually happens.

Unexpected: this is something that happens a lot around horses, i.e. what you assumed would happen doesn't happen, something else does instead!

Paradox: apparently contradictory views of something, that are both apparently right!

Index